Testing and Securing Android Studio Applications

Debug and secure your Android applications with Android Studio

Belén Cruz Zapata

Antonio Hernández Niñirola

[PACKT] open source*
PUBLISHING   community experience distilled

BIRMINGHAM - MUMBAI

Testing and Securing Android Studio Applications

First published: August 2014

Production reference: 1190814

Published by Packt Publishing Ltd.
Livery Place
35 Livery Street
Birmingham B3 2PB, UK.

ISBN 978-1-78398-880-8

www.packtpub.com

Cover image by Ravaji Babu (ravaji_babu@outlook.com)

Credits

Authors

Belén Cruz Zapata

Antonio Hernández Niñirola

Reviewers

Nico Küchler

Anand Mohan

Ravi Shanker

Kevin Smith

Abhinava Srivastava

Commissioning Editor

Amarabha Banerjee

Acquisition Editor

Rebecca Youé

Content Development Editor

Parita Khedekar

Technical Editor

Mrunmayee Patil

Copy Editors

Roshni Banerjee

Adithi Shetty

Project Coordinators

Neha Thakur

Amey Sawant

Proofreader

Ameesha Green

Indexers

Mariammal Chettiyar

Rekha Nair

Tejal Soni

Priya Subramani

Graphics

Ronak Dhruv

Production Coordinator

Conidon Miranda

Cover Work

Conidon Miranda

About the Authors

Belén Cruz Zapata received her engineering degree in Computer Science from the University of Murcia in Spain, with specialization in software technologies and intelligent and knowledge technologies. She has earned an MSc degree in Computer Science and is now working on her PhD degree in Software Engineering Research Group from the University of Murcia.

Belén is based in Spain; however, due to the field of her PhD, she is now collaborating with Université Mohammed V - Soussi in Rabat. Her research is focused on mobile technologies in general and also applies to medicine.

Belén has worked as a mobile developer for several platforms, such as Android, iOS, and the Web. She is the author of the book on Android Studio: *Android Studio Application Development, Packt Publishing*.

To follow her projects, she maintains a blog at `http://www.belencruz.com` and you can follow her on Twitter at `@belen_cz`.

I would like to thank Packt Publishing for offering me the opportunity to write this book. I would particularly like to thank Parita Khedekar, Rebecca Youé, and Amey Sawant for their valuable help.

I would also like to thank Antonio, the co-author of this book, for making everything so easy; my new friends of adventure, especially Paloma, Camilla, and Adrián, for these last months; my friends from way back for visiting me; and finally, my family for supporting me.

Antonio Hernández Niñirola has an engineering degree in Computer Science and is a mobile application developer. He was born and raised in Murcia in the southeast region of Spain and is currently living in Rabat, Morocco. He has developed several websites and mobile applications.

After completing his degree in Computer Science, he pursued a Master's degree in Teacher Training for Informatics and Technology. Antonio pushed his studies further and is now a doctoral candidate under the Software Engineering Research Group of the faculty of Computer Science at the University of Murcia, and is actually a researcher for the Université Mohammed V - Soussi in Rabat.

You can visit his website at `http://www.ninirola.es` to find out more about him and his projects.

I would like to begin by thanking Rebecca Youé, Parita Khedekar, and Amey Sawant for their valuable input. Thank you to everyone at Packt Publishing who make writing a book such an enjoyable experience.

Thank you Belén, the other half of this book, for making everything much better. I would finally like to thank my family for their support, my new friends in Morocco, my old friends in Spain, and everyone who helped me be who I am today.

About the Reviewers

Nico Küchler lives in Berlin, Germany. He did an apprenticeship as a mathematical-technical software developer. He has worked for the gamble industry and as an online shop provider. He has been working at Deutsche Post E-POST Development GmbH for 2 years within the scope of Android app development.

He has been maintaining a project that provides a quick start with test-driven Android app development at `https://github.com/nenick/android-gradle-template`.

Anand Mohan is a geek and a start-up enthusiast. He graduated from the Indian Institute of Information Technology, Allahabad, in 2008. He has worked with Oracle India Pvt. Ltd. for 4 years. In 2012, Anand started his own venture, TripTern, along with his friends, which is a company that algorithmically plans out the most optimized travel itinerary for travelers by utilizing Big Data and machine-learning algorithms. At TripTern, Anand has developed and implemented offline Android applications so that travelers can modify their itinerary on the go without relying on any data plan.

Apart from working on his start-up, Anand also likes to follow the latest trends in technology and best security practices.

Ravi Shanker has always been fascinated with technology. He's been a passionate practitioner and an avid follower of the digital revolution. He lives in Sydney, Australia. He loves traveling, presenting, reading, and listening to music. When not tinkering with the technology, he also wields a set of brushes and palette of colors to put the right side of his brain to work.

Ravi has honed his skills over a decade in development, consulting, and product and project management for start-ups to large corporations in airline, transportation, telecom, media, and financial services. He has worked in the USA, UK, Australia, Japan, and most of Asia-Pacific. He has also run a couple of start-ups of his own in the past.

Ravi is often seen blogging, answering or asking questions on Stack Exchange, posting or upvoting, and tweeting on the latest developments in digital space. He has made presentations at meetings and interest groups and has conducted training classes on various technologies. He's always excited at the prospect of new and innovative developments in improving the quality of life.

Abhinava Srivastava has completed his Bachelor of Technology degree in Computer Science Engineering from India in 2008 and has also received a Diploma in Wireless and Mobile Computing from ACTS, C-DAC, India in 2009.

He started his career as a Software Engineer at Persistent Systems before moving to Singapore, and is currently working with MasterCard, Singapore.

Abhinava is a core technologist by heart and loves to play with open source technologies. He maintains his own blog at `http://abhinavasblog.blogspot.in/` and keeps jotting his thoughts from time to time.

I would like to thank my family members for their continuous support, especially my elder brother, Abhishek Srivastava, who has been a mentor and an inspiration. Last but not least, I would like to extend my gratitude to Packt Publishing for giving me the opportunity to be a part of such a wonderful experience.

www.PacktPub.com

Support files, eBooks, discount offers, and more

You might want to visit www.PacktPub.com for support files and downloads related to your book.

Did you know that Packt offers eBook versions of every book published, with PDF and ePub files available? You can upgrade to the eBook version at www.PacktPub.com and as a print book customer, you are entitled to a discount on the eBook copy. Get in touch with us at service@packtpub.com for more details.

At www.PacktPub.com, you can also read a collection of free technical articles, sign up for a range of free newsletters, and receive exclusive discounts and offers on Packt books and eBooks.

http://PacktLib.PacktPub.com

Do you need instant solutions to your IT questions? PacktLib is Packt's online digital book library. Here, you can access, read and search across Packt's entire library of books.

Why subscribe?

- Fully searchable across every book published by Packt
- Copy and paste, print and bookmark content
- On demand and accessible via web browser

Free access for Packt account holders

If you have an account with Packt at www.PacktPub.com, you can use this to access PacktLib today and view nine entirely free books. Simply use your login credentials for immediate access.

Table of Contents

Preface

Mobile applications have become very popular in the last few years thanks to a huge increment in the use of mobile devices. From a developer's point of view, Android has become an important source of income thanks to the different app repositories, such as Google Play and Amazon Appstore.

With an increase in the number of applications available, users have become more demanding about the features of the applications they are going to use. A solid testing of the application and its security aspects are the key factors in the pursuit of success for an application. Bugs and security issues are obviously not features that help your application do well in the increasingly more exigent market of Android.

In this book, you are going to learn how to turn your Android application into a solidly debugged and secure application. To achieve this, you will learn how to use Android Studio and its most important features: testing and security.

What this book covers

Chapter 1, *Introduction to Software Security*, introduces the principles of software security.

Chapter 2, *Security in Android Applications*, describes the distinctive features found in mobile environments and the Android system.

Chapter 3, *Monitoring Your Application*, presents the debugging environment, one of the most important features of an IDE.

Chapter 4, *Mitigating Vulnerabilities*, describes the measures that should be taken to prevent attacks.

Chapter 5, *Preserving Data Privacy*, presents the mechanisms offered by Android to preserve the privacy of user data.

Chapter 6, *Securing Communications*, explains the mechanisms offered by Android to secure communications between an Android application and an external server.

Chapter 7, *Authentication Methods*, presents different types of authentication methods used in Android mobile devices.

Chapter 8, *Testing Your Application*, introduces ways to test an application using Android Studio.

Chapter 9, *Unit and Functional Tests*, covers unit and functional tests that allow developers to quickly verify the state and behavior of an activity on its own.

Chapter 10, *Supporting Tools*, presents a set of external tools different from Android Studio to help developers test an Android application.

Chapter 11, *Further Considerations*, provides some further considerations that are useful for developers.

What you need for this book

For this book, you need a computer with a Windows, Mac OS, or Linux system. You will also need to have Java and the Android Studio IDE installed on your system.

Who this book is for

This book is a guide for developers with some Android knowledge, but who do not know how to test their applications using Android Studio. This book is suitable for developers who have knowledge about software security but not about security in mobile applications, and also for developers who do not have any knowledge about software security. It's assumed that you are familiar with Android and it is also recommended to be familiar with the Android Studio IDE.

Conventions

In this book, you will find a number of text styles that will help you distinguish between different kinds of information. Here are some examples of these styles and an explanation of their meaning.

Code words in text, database table names, folder names, filenames, file extensions, pathnames, dummy URLs, user input, and Twitter handles are shown as follows: "To send an ordered broadcast, you can call the `sendOrderedBroadcast` method."

A block of code is set as follows:

```
Instrumentation.ActivityMonitor monitor =
   getInstrumentation().addMonitor(
   SecondActivity.class.getName(), null, false);
```

When we wish to draw your attention to a particular part of a code block, the relevant lines or items are set in bold:

```
@Override
protected void setUp() throws Exception {
super.setUp();

Intent intent = new
   Intent(getInstrumentation().getTargetContext(),
   MainActivity.class);
startActivity(intent, null, null);
mActivity = getActivity();
```

Any command-line input or output is written as follows:

```
adb shell monkey -p com.packt.package -v 100
```

New terms and **important words** are shown in bold. Words that you see on the screen, in menus or dialog boxes for example, appear in the text like this: "The multiplication is made when the **Button1** button is clicked."

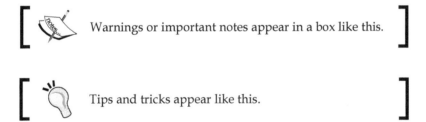

> Warnings or important notes appear in a box like this.

> Tips and tricks appear like this.

Reader feedback

Feedback from our readers is always welcome. Let us know what you think about this book—what you liked or may have disliked. Reader feedback is important for us to develop titles that you really get the most out of.

To send us general feedback, simply send an e-mail to feedback@packtpub.com, and mention the book title through the subject of your message.

If there is a topic that you have expertise in and you are interested in either writing or contributing to a book, see our author guide on www.packtpub.com/authors.

Customer support

Now that you are the proud owner of a Packt book, we have a number of things to help you to get the most from your purchase.

Downloading the example code

You can download the example code files for all Packt books you have purchased from your account at http://www.packtpub.com. If you purchased this book elsewhere, you can visit http://www.packtpub.com/support and register to have the files e-mailed directly to you.

Errata

Although we have taken every care to ensure the accuracy of our content, mistakes do happen. If you find a mistake in one of our books—maybe a mistake in the text or the code—we would be grateful if you would report this to us. By doing so, you can save other readers from frustration and help us improve subsequent versions of this book. If you find any errata, please report them by visiting http://www.packtpub.com/support, selecting your book, clicking on the **errata submission form** link, and entering the details of your errata. Once your errata are verified, your submission will be accepted and the errata will be uploaded to our website, or added to any list of existing errata, under the Errata section of that title.

Piracy

Piracy of copyright material on the Internet is an ongoing problem across all media. At Packt, we take the protection of our copyright and licenses very seriously. If you come across any illegal copies of our works, in any form, on the Internet, please provide us with the location address or website name immediately so that we can pursue a remedy.

Please contact us at copyright@packtpub.com with a link to the suspected pirated material.

We appreciate your help in protecting our authors, and our ability to bring you valuable content.

Questions

You can contact us at questions@packtpub.com if you are having a problem with any aspect of the book, and we will do our best to address it.

1
Introduction to Software Security

You want to learn how to improve your Android applications so that they're secure and robust. You would like to learn about mobile software security and its most important threats and vulnerabilities. You want your users to be satisfied while ensuring that their data is secure and that the application has no bugs. Can you do this easily? What do you need to do in order to achieve this?

This chapter will teach you the basics of software security. We'll begin by teaching you the different security terms that we will use in this book. You'll see the most important threats and vulnerabilities that may affect your application. You'll then learn about secure code design principles, as well as how to test our application for security issues.

In this chapter, we will cover the following topics:

- Software security terms
- Threats, vulnerabilities, and risks
- Secure code design principles
- Security testing

Software security terms

In recent years, the Internet has experienced a huge increase in **electronic commerce** (**e-commerce**). This increase in monetization of information in the cloud means that attackers can now be rewarded financially, socially, and even politically for a successful attack. There is a low risk in attempting these attacks, since there is a small chance of getting captured and therefore, of prosecution. With a more motivated enemy, companies and enterprises have to improve their security measures to face these new threats. They must identify the threats and defend the vulnerabilities that may affect the data that has a big impact on their business.

In order to understand the content of this book completely, you will first need to understand some basic concepts about software security:

- **Access control**: This ensures selective access to resources by users that are entitled to it.

- **Asymmetric cryptography**: This is also known as the public key cryptography and uses algorithms that employ a pair of keys — one public and one private. A public key is used to encrypt the data while a private key is used to decrypt data.

- **Authentication**: This is a process through which we can confirm the identity of a user.

- **Authorization**: This is a process through which we give someone permission to do or have something.

- **Availability**: This means that the system and data are available to authorized users when they may make use of it.

- **Brute force**: This is a very basic and nonoptimal cryptanalysis technique that tries every possibility to crack a key or a password.

- **Cipher**: This is a cryptographic algorithm that may be used for encryption and decryption.

- **Code injection**: This is an attack where the code is inserted into application queries. This kind of attack is commonly used to alter databases via SQL injections.

- **Confidentiality**: This specifies that the data is only available for users who have permission to access it.

- **Crack**: This is the process through which an attacker attempts to gain access to a machine, network, or software.

- **Decryption**: This is the process through which an encrypted message is transformed into its original state.

- **Denial-of-service (DoS)**: This is a type of attack that makes an online resource unavailable for a fixed amount of time.

- **Distributed denial-of-service (DDoS)**: This type of attack is similar to the DoS attack, but it is perpetrated from several machines and is generally more effective than a DoS attack.

- **Dictionary attack**: This is a basic cryptanalysis technique that uses all the words in a dictionary when trying to crack a key or password.

- **Encryption**: This is a process through which a plain piece of data is transformed into an encrypted state, with the objective of concealing this information in order to prevent access from unwanted sources.

- **Hash function**: This is a type of algorithm that maps data of different sizes into data of a fixed size.

- **Hijack attack**: This is a form of attack in which an already established communication is seized and acts as one of the original participants.

- **Hypertext Transfer Protocol Secure (HTTPS)**: This is an application level protocol based on HTTP that allows a secure transfer of sensitive information in the form of hypertext.

- **Integrity**: This means that the information is accurate and is not changed accidentally or deliberately.

- **MD5**: This is a very commonly used hash function.

- **Man-in-the-middle attack**: This is a type of attack where the attacker assumes a position in the middle of a communication, intercepts and reads the messages of a communication, and lets the victims believe that they are directly connected to each other.

- **Password**: This is a string of characters used for authentication.

- **Phishing**: This is an attack attempt that appears to be from a reliable source and tricks the user into entering their authentication credentials in a different domain or application.

- **Risk**: This is the likelihood of an attack happening and succeeding.

- **SHA1**: This is a commonly used hash function.

- **Sniffing attack**: This is an attack that analyses the packets exchanged in a network in order to extract useful information from them.

- **Spoofing attack**: This is an attack where an unauthorized entity gains access to a system with the credentials of an authorized user.

- **Symmetric cryptography**: This is a type of cryptography that uses the same key for encryption and decryption, and therefore, every entity shares the same key.

- **Threat**: This is a circumstance that could breach security and cause harm to the system.
- **Vulnerability**: This is a weakness that allows for a threat to occur.

Threats, vulnerabilities, and risks

There are three key terms that you need to understand. They were defined in the previous section, but we will talk a little bit more about them since they are commonly mixed up. These terms are threat, risk, and vulnerability and they are discussed in the following sections.

Threat

A threat is anything that may exploit vulnerability in order to access, modify, or destroy information. A threat is the source and type of an attack and is what we try to defend against. Threat assessments are used to determine the best way to defend against a determined class of threat.

When we consider a communication between two authorized entities, a source (**S**) and a destination (**D**), threats can be categorized into the following four segments:

- **Interception**: This happens when an attacking entity has an access to a communication between two authorized entities. The entities do not realize that interception is happening and keep on with their communication normally.
- **Interruption**: This refers to when the attacking entity intercepts the communication. The source entity may not realize this is happening, while the destination entity has no knowledge of the communication attempt.
- **Modification**: This happens when the attacking entity changes the information sent between the two authorized entities. The destination entity does not realize that the information has been tampered with by the attacking entity.
- **Fabrication**: This happens when the attacking entity acts like the source entity. The destination entity acknowledges the communication as if it was produced by the source entity.

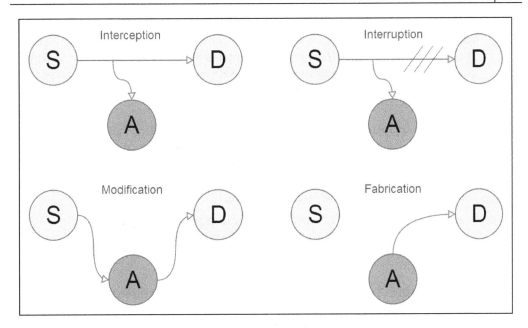

Vulnerability

Vulnerability is a weakness or a flaw in the security system of our application that may be used by a determined threat to access, modify, or destroy information. Vulnerability testing is mandatory and should be performed repeatedly to ensure the security of our application.

When a human or a system tries to exploit vulnerability, it is considered to be an attack. Some of the most common kinds of vulnerabilities that can be exploited to damage our system are as follows:

- **Improper authentication**: This happens when an entity claims that it has been authenticated and the software does not check whether this is true or false. This vulnerability affects our system of access control, since an attacker can evade the authentication process. A very common example of exploiting this vulnerability is modifying a cookie which has a field that determines whether the user is logged in. Setting `loggedin` to `true` can cheat the system into believing that the entity is already logged in and is therefore granted access when it should not be granted.

- **Buffer overflow**: This happens when the software has access to a determined amount of memory but tries to read a buffer out of the limits. For example, if the software has a buffer of size N but tries to read the position $N+2$, it will read information that may be used by another process. This grants access and even modifies the information that belongs to a part of the memory where the software should not have access.

- **Cross-site scripting (XSS)**: This is a kind of vulnerability that allows a third-party to inject code in our software. It is especially common in websites, but it also applies to certain mobile applications. The most commonly used examples of XSS are the access to cookies from a different site and the injection of JavaScript into a different site.

- **Input validation**: When reading information provided by the user, it is always a good idea to validate the data. Not validating the data may result in an attacker introducing certain unexpected values that can cause an issue in the system.

- **SQL injection**: This is a kind of input validation vulnerability. It is very common to use a search feature in almost any application. The string that the user introduces in the search field is then introduced in a SQL sentence. If there is no analysis and filter of the string provided by the user, an attacker could write a SQL query that would be executed. If this is combined with a bad access control, the attacker could even delete the whole database.

Risk

A risk is the potential for an attack happening and being successful. The more sensitive the information, the higher the risk of attack, as it can cause a higher level of damage to our system. Risks are the result of a threat exploiting vulnerability and accessing, modifying, or destroying a piece of information that we want to be protected. Risk assessments are performed to identify the most critical dangers and to evaluate the potential damage. This potential damage is calculated through a state between the cost of a breach happening, which depends on how sensitive the information is, and the probability of that event, which depends on the threats and vulnerabilities that may affect the application.

As you can see, there is a very important relationship between these three terms; especially when trying to correctly identify the risk that the information stored suffers. Assessing threats and detecting vulnerabilities is crucial to the protection of the information in our application.

Secure code-design principles

In order to reduce the number of vulnerabilities of your application, a good security design is mandatory. There are many standards and guidelines that recommend different processes to produce secure applications. In this section, we are going to identify the most important principles that you should follow when designing your application:

- **Secure defaults**: Security is of the utmost importance for an average user. When designing your application, you should make sure that the most demanding user is going to be satisfied and, therefore, your application should offer the best security methods available. However, there are some users who may prefer accessibility over security and may want to reduce the level of security. For example, you may want to add password aging to your authentication system. This means that every established period of time, the users should change their password to a new one. This means an additional level of security but can be annoying for certain users. Adding an option in the preferences to turn off this feature can be a good idea. However, always make sure to set the default to the more secure setting, and let the user decide whether they want to increase the risk of breaching their information.

- **Least privileges**: Privileges are sometimes conceded in excess in order to speed up the process of development. This principle states that you should always concede the least privileges as possible in order to minimize security risks.

- **Clarity**: Never trust obscurity to ensure the security of your application. Concealing the information on how your security system works is a good idea, but it should not be granted as enough by itself; the security must come from good cryptographic techniques and a good security design.

- **Small surface area**: If you know you may have vulnerability in a determined section of your code, you can try to minimize the risk of a threat exploiting it by minimizing the overall use of this section. For example, if you think that certain functionality may be exploited, you can restrict this functionality to authenticated users.

- **Strong defense**: When defending against a certain attack, there may be different methods to use. One control can surely be enough but sensitive information demands extraordinary measures. Also, using more than one method of precaution is most of the times convenient.

- **Failing securely**: When developing our application, we aim for the highest robustness. However, applications fail sometimes and we need to adapt our code to make sure the application fails securely. When programming for Android, we can address this issue by controlling every exception, for example, through the correct usage of `try` and `catch`.

- **Not trusting the third-party companies**: There are many services available that have been developed by the third-party companies with different privacy and security policies. It is important to know that while using one of these services, you trust the companies on how they use your information. The principle of not trusting the third-party companies recommends that you should only trust an external service with the minimal amount of information possible and always implies a certain level of trust with them.

- **Simplicity**: Always try to keep your security code simple. Although it is recommended to use code patterns, when talking about security, the safest and more robust way is its simplicity.

- **Address vulnerabilities**: When you detect vulnerability, it is important to address this issue correctly. You need to understand both the vulnerability and the threat and then act accordingly.

Testing the basics

As stated by Boris Beizer, author of the book *Software Testing Techniques*, *Dreamtech Press*:

> *"Bugs lurk in corners and congregate at boundaries."*

Security testing can be defined as a process through which we find vulnerabilities or flaws in our security system. Although we may do exhaustive security testing, it does not imply that no flaws exist. In this section, we will focus on the taxonomy of tests that can be performed in any circumstance.

Tests can be categorized into two big groups: white-box tests or structural tests and black-box tests or functional tests. Structural testing, more commonly known as the white-box testing, is a testing method that evaluates the internal behavior of a component. It is focused on the analysis of the behavior of each procedure in different moments of execution. The white-box test evaluates how the software produces a result. Functional testing, specification testing, or black-box testing, are methods of testing that focus on the functionality of the component rather than its structure. When using this kind of test, the tester is aware that a certain input should generate a particular output. This test evaluates what the software produces.

The two test categories, white-box test and black-box test, are shown in the following diagrams:

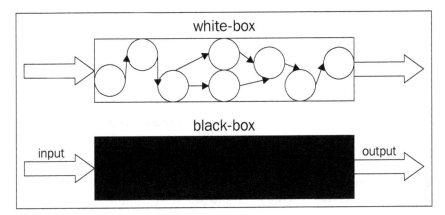

There are various white-box techniques. However, the most commonly used are control flow testing, data flow testing, basis path testing, and statement coverage and they are explained as follows:

- **Control flow testing**: This evaluates the flow graph of the software to indicate whether the set of tests covers every possible test case.

- **Data flow testing**: This requires an evaluation of how the program variables are used.

- **Basis path testing**: This ensures that every possible path in a code has been included in the test cases.

- **Statement coverage**: This consists of the evaluation of the code and the development of individual tests that will work on every individual line of code.

The black-box testing design also includes different techniques. The most frequently used techniques are equivalence partitioning, boundary value analysis, cause-effect graphing, state transition testing, all pairs testing, and syntax testing, and they are explained as follows:

- **Equivalence partitioning**: This divides test cases in different partitions that present similar characteristics. This technique can help in reducing the number of tests cases.

- **Boundary value analysis**: This is performed in order to analyze the behavior of a component when the input is near the extreme valid values.

- **Cause-effect graphing**: This graphically illustrates the relationship between circumstances or events that cause a determined effect on the system.

- **State transition testing**: This is performed through a number of inputs that make the system execute valid or invalid state transitions.

- **All pairs testing**: This is a combinatorial method that tests every possible combination of parameters. When the number of parameters and the possible values for each parameter are big, this test technique can be combined with the equivalent partitioning technique to reduce the number of test cases.

- **Syntax testing**: This analyses the specifications of a component to evaluate its behavior with a huge number of different inputs. This process is usually automatized due to the large number of inputs required.

When testing an application, there are different levels of testing that depend on the size of the part of the system involved. There are five commonly known levels of tests: unit, integration, validation, system, and acceptance.

- **Unit tests**: These tests focus on each individual component. These tests are usually performed by the same development team and consist of a series of tests that evaluate the behavior of a single component checking for the correctness of the data and its integrity.

- **Integration tests**: These tests are performed by the development team. These tests assess the communication between different components.

- **Validation tests**: These tests are performed by the fully developed software in order to evaluate the fulfilment of functional and performance requirements. They can also be used to assess how easy it is to maintain or to see how the software manages errors.

- **System tests**: These tests involve the whole system. Once the software is validated, it is integrated in the system.

- **Acceptance tests**: These tests are performed in the real environment where the software is used. The user performs these tests and accepts the final product.

The higher the level of testing, unit testing being the lowest and acceptance testing the highest, the more likely it is to use black-box tests. Unit tests evaluate components that are small and therefore easy to analyze in behavior. However, the higher the level, the bigger the system, and therefore the more difficult and more resource-consuming it is to apply white-box testing category. This does not mean that you should not apply the black-box testing category while performing unit tests, as each one complements the other.

Summary

In this chapter, learned the basic and most commonly used terminologies while discussing software security. You know the difference between threat, vulnerability, and risk, and understand how each one is related to the other. You also learned about the different kinds of threats and vulnerabilities that can affect a system. You now know how to properly approach coding your security system thanks to the secure code principles. Finally, you learned about the different methods of testing that you should consider in order to make your application robust. Properly understanding these definitions allows you to design better security systems for your software.

So as a developer, you have to address the security of your application, but what does Android do for you? Android has several built-in security measures that reduce the frequency and the potential damage that application security issues may cause. In the next chapter, you will learn about these features and understand how they work.

2
Security in Android Applications

You understand the security concepts in software and now you want to discover how those threats and vulnerabilities are applied to a mobile environment. You want to be aware of the special security features in the Android operating system. You are already familiar with Android, but you need to know the components that are critical for its security.

This chapter will show you the challenges that exist in the mobile environment. You will learn about the Android security architecture and about what application sandboxing means. This chapter will show you the main features in Android that will allow you protect your location: permissions and interprocess communication.

We will be covering the following topics in this chapter:

- Vulnerabilities in the mobile environment
- Android security overview
- Permissions
- Interapplication communication

The mobile environment

Android is an **operating system** (**OS**) created for intelligent mobile devices with a touchscreen, such as smartphones or tablets. Knowing the features of a device is important to identify the vulnerabilities that can potentially compromise the integrity, confidentiality, or availability of your **application** (**app**).

A smartphone is a connected device and so malicious software can infect it in several ways. The smartphone can communicate with different devices by a wireless or wired connection. For example, it can connect to a computer by a cable or it can connect to another mobile device by a wireless Bluetooth network. These communications allow the user to transfer data, files, or software, which is a possible path to infect the smartphone with malware.

A smartphone is also a connected device in the sense that it can connect to the Internet by cellular networks like 3G or access points via Wi-Fi. Internet is therefore another path of potential threats to the security of smartphones.

Smartphones also have internal vulnerabilities, for example, malicious apps that are installed by the user themselves. These malicious apps can collect the smartphone's data without the user's knowledge. Sensitive data might be exposed because of implementation errors or because of errors that occur while sending data to the wrong receiver. Communication between the apps installed in the smartphone can become a way to attack them.

The following figure represents the types of existing vulnerabilities in smartphones. The connection to the network is one of the external vulnerabilities, since network connections are susceptible to sniffing or spoofing attacks. The connections to external devices also involve potential vulnerabilities as mentioned earlier. Regarding internal vulnerabilities, implementation errors can cause failures and attackers can take advantage of them. Finally, user unawareness is also a vulnerability that affects the internals of the smartphone. For example, installing apps from untrusted sources or setting an imprudent configuration for Wi-Fi or Bluetooth services is a risk.

As a developer, you cannot control the risks associated with external devices or the network, not even those related to user unawareness. Therefore, your responsibility is to create robust apps without implementation errors that can cause security breaches.

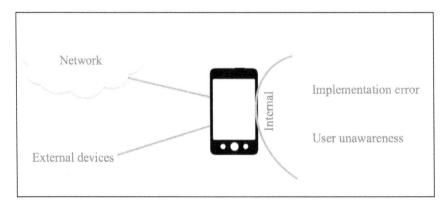

An overview of Android security

Android provides a secure architecture to protect the system and its applications. Android architecture is structured like a software stack in which each component of a layer accepts that the layer following it is secure. The following figure shows a simplified version of the Android security architecture:

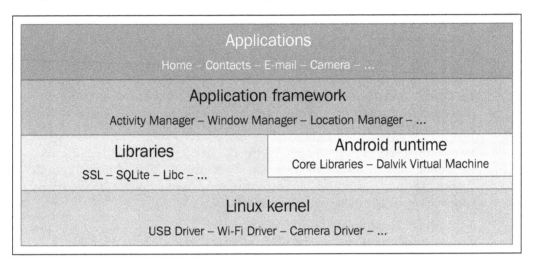

Android OS is a multiuser, Linux-based platform in which each app has a different user. Each app has its own **user ID (UID)** in the Linux kernel that is unique. The UID is assigned by the system and is unknown to the app. Because of the unique UID, Android apps run in separate processes with different permissions. This mechanism is known as **application sandboxing**. The **Android Application Sandbox** isolates each application's data and code execution to improve its security and prevent malware. This means that under normal circumstances, you cannot have access to other application's data and other applications do not have access to your application's data. As the Application Sandbox is implemented in the Linux kernel, the security provided by this mechanism is extended to all the layers above the kernel (such as libraries, Android runtime, application framework, and application runtime). For example, if a memory corruption error is generated, this error will only have consequences for the application in which the error was produced.

Application sandboxing is one of the main security features of Android, but we can also find the following features in the security model:

- **Application-defined permissions**: If applications are isolated from each other, how can they share information when required? Applications can define permissions to allow other applications to control its data. There are also many predefined system-based permissions cover many situations and that will reduce the necessity of creating permissions, especially for your application.

- **Interprocess communication**: Under normal circumstances, every component of an application runs in the same process. However, there are times when developers decide to run certain components in different processes. Android provides an interprocess communication method that is secure and robust.

- **Support for secure networking**: Network transactions are especially risky on mobile devices that commonly use unsecured Wi-Fi networks in public spaces. Android supports the most commonly used protocols to secure connections under these extreme conditions.

- **Support for cryptography**: Android provides a framework that developers can use with tested and robust implementations of commonly used cryptographic methods.

- **Encrypted file system**: Android provides a full filesystem encryption. This means that the information stored on an Android device is encrypted and is therefore protected at any time against external entities. This option is not active by default and requires a username and a password.

- **Application signing**: The installation package of every app must be signed with a certificate, which can be a self-signed certificate. An attacker can preserve their anonymity, since it's not necessary for a trusted third-party to sign the certificate. Certificates are mainly used to distinguish developers and allow the system to manage permissions. To prevent an attacker from modifying your application, you should keep your certificate safe. Furthermore, application updates must be signed with this same certificate.

Permissions

With application sandboxing, apps cannot access parts of the system without permission, but even with it, Android allows data sharing with other apps or access to some system services. An app needs to request permission to access device data or to access system services. Permissions are a security feature of Android system, but misused permissions make your application vulnerable.

The permission needs of an app are declared in its manifest file. This manifest file is bundled into the app's **Android application package (APK)**, which includes its compiled code along with other resources. The permissions requested in the manifest file (manifest permissions) will be shown to the user when installing the app. The user should review these permissions and accept them to complete the installation process. If the user agrees to them, the protected resources are available to the app.

[Do not request permissions that your app does not need. Reducing the number of permissions makes your app less vulnerable.]

Permissions control how an app interacts with the system by using an Android **application programming interface (API)**. Some of the protected APIs that need permission include the following:

- Bluetooth
- Camera
- Location GPS
- Network and data connections
- NFC
- SMS and MMS
- Telephony

For example, to request permission to use the camera, you have to add the following line code in our manifest file:

```
<uses-permission android:name="android.permission.CAMERA" />
```

The following code is used to request permission to access the Internet:

```
<uses-permission android:name="android.permission.INTERNET" />
```

The following code is used to request permission to send a SMS:

```
<uses-permission android:name="android.permission.SEND_SMS" />
```

Interapplication communication

Apps in Android cannot access each other's data directly because of application sandboxing, but Android's system provides some other mechanisms for the applications to communicate with each other. Intents and content providers are mechanisms that we can use on the Java API layer. Intents and content providers should be used carefully to prevent attacks from malware applications. This is the reason why it is important to understand their characteristics.

Intents

Intents are an asynchronous interprocess communication mechanism. Intent is a message that includes the receiver and optional arguments to pass the data. The receiver of Intent can be declared explicitly so that the Intent is sent to a particular component, or it can be declared implicitly so that the Intent is sent to any component that can handle it. Intents are used for intra-application communication (in the same application), or for interapplication communication (in different applications). The following components can receive Intents:

- **Activities**: An activity represents a screen in the app. Intents can start activities, and these activities can return data to the invoking component. To start an activity using Intent, you can call the `startActivity` method or the `startActivityForResult` method to receive a result from the activity.

- **Services**: A service performs long-running background tasks without interacting with the user. To start a service using Intent, you can call the `startService` method or the `bindService` method to bind other components to it.

- **Broadcast receivers**: Intents can be sent to multiple receivers through broadcast receivers. When a receiver is started because of Intent, it runs in the background and often delivers the message to an activity or a service. Some system events generate broadcast messages to notify you, for example, when the device starts charging or when the device's battery level is low. To send a broadcast message using Intent, you can call the `sendBroadcast` method. To send an ordered broadcast, you can call the `sendOrderedBroadcast` method. To send a sticky broadcast, you can call the `sendStickyBroadcast` method. There are three types of broadcast messages:

- ° **Normal broadcast**: In this type of broadcast, the message is delivered to all the receivers at the same time. Soon after, the message is no longer available.

- ° **Ordered broadcast**: In this type of broadcast, the message is delivered to one receiver at a time depending on its priority level. Any receiver can stop the propagation of the message to the rest of the receivers. Soon after, the message is no longer available.

- ° **Sticky broadcast**: In this type of broadcast, the message is sent but it does not disappear. An example of a sticky broadcast is the battery level. An app can find out which was the last battery level broadcast because it remains accessible.

Application communication by Intents allows the receiver and optional arguments to reuse each other's features. For example, if you want to show a web page in your app, you can create Intent to start any activity that is able to handle it. You do not need to implement the functionality to display a web page in our app. The following code shows you how to create Intent to display web page content:

```
Intent i = new Intent(Intent.ACTION_VIEW);
i.setData(Uri.parse("http://www.packtpub.com"));
startActivity(i);
```

Downloading the example code

You can download the example code files for all Packt books you have purchased from your account at http://www.packtpub.com. If you purchased this book elsewhere, you can visit http://www.packtpub.com/support and register to have the files e-mailed directly to you.

The preceding code is an example of an implicit Intent in which a general action is indicated: Intent.ACTION_VIEW. The Android system searches for all the apps that match the Intent. If there is more than one application that matches the Intent and the user has not set a default one, a dialog is displayed so that the user can choose which one of them to use.

Intents that are supported by a component are declared in the manifest file using the Intent filters. The broadcast receivers can be also be declared at runtime. Intent filter declares the types of Intents that a component can respond to. When a component includes an Intent filter, the component is exported so it can receive Intents from other components. Intent filter can constrict by the action of the Intent, by the type of data, or by the category of the Intent. For example, if you want your app to behave as a browser, you have to create an activity with the following Intent filters in your manifest file:

```
<activity …>
  <intent-filter>
    <action android:name="android.intent.action.VIEW" />
    <data android:scheme="http" />
    <category android:name="android.intent.category.DEFAULT" />
    <category android:name="android.intent.category.BROWSABLE" />
  </intent-filter>
</activity>
```

The following example shows you how to register a receiver to run when the device starts charging:

```
<receiver…>
  <intent-filter>
    <action android:name=
      "android.intent.action.ACTION_POWER_CONNECTED" />
  </intent-filter>
</receiver>
```

 If you want to learn more about Intents, you might want to check out the official documentation: http://developer.android.com/guide/components/intents-filters.html.

Content providers

Content providers are a mechanism that allows sharing between applications and serves as persistent internal data storage facility. The data stored through a content provider is structured and the interface is designed to be used with a **Structural Query Language (SQL)** backend. Although it is common to use a SQL database behind content providers, file storage or REST calls can also be used. If you are not familiar with content providers, you might want to check out the official documentation since it is a broad topic: `http://developer.android.com/guide/topics/providers/content-providers.html`. Our interest in content providers is related to their security and permissions. Content providers are the perfect scenario for SQL injection attacks.

To access the data of content providers, there are content resolvers that you can use in your app. The provider's data is identified by a content URI. To access the content provider, you should use the `getContentResolver().query()` method, which receives the following parameters:

- **Content URI**: This is the URI that identifies the data (the FROM clause in SQL)
- **Projection**: This specifies the columns to retrieve for each row (the SELECT clause in SQL)
- **Selection**: This is the criteria to select the rows (the WHERE clause in SQL)
- **Selection arguments**: This complements the criteria to select the rows
- **Sort order**: This is the sort order for the rows (the ORDER BY clause in SQL)

There are some content providers offered by the Android system itself, such as the calendar provider and the contacts provider. To access the system content providers, you need to request the permission in your manifest file. For example, to be able to read the contacts, you must add the following permission to your app:

```
<uses-permission android:name="android.permission.READ_CONTACTS" />
```

To acquire the writing access permissions, you must add the following line of code in your manifest:

```
<uses-permission android:name="android.permission.WRITE_CONTACTS" />
```

Any other content provider, not only those of the system, can indicate the required permissions that other apps must request so that they can access the provider's data.

Summary

In this chapter, you learned about the vulnerabilities associated with mobile devices—both external and internal. You now understand the Android architecture and the features provided by the system to keep it safe. You now know which components of the Java API layer are vulnerable to attacks, so you can learn how to mitigate them in the next chapters of this book.

In the next chapter, we will start using Android Studio IDE. As the first step to create secure Android applications, you will learn how to monitor Android applications in the debugging environment in order to detect incorrect behaviors.

Monitoring Your Application

3

You are now aware of the importance of learning how to monitor the activity of your Android application and are also familiar with the basic console or logs that you use to debug your application. However, there is more to learn about the debugging tool available in Android Studio. Android Studio includes the **Dalvik Debug Monitor Server (DDMS)** debugging tool. Do you want to use this debugging tool while programming in Android Studio?

This chapter presents the debugging environment, one of the most important features of an IDE. Monitoring your Android application allows you to detect the incorrect behaviors and security vulnerabilities. In this chapter, you will learn about the information available in the advanced debugging tool included in Android Studio: DDMS.

The topics that will be covered in this chapter are as follows:

- Debugging and DDMS
- Thread and method profiling
- Heap usage and memory allocation
- Network statistics
- File explorer
- Emulator control and system information

Debugging and DDMS

In Android Studio, you can use different mechanisms to debug your application. One of them is the **debugger**. The debugger manages the breakpoints, controls the execution of the code, and displays information about the variables. To debug an application, navigate to **Run | Debug 'MyApplication'** or click on the bug icon present in the toolbar.

Another mechanism is the **Console**. The Console displays the events that are taking place while the application is being launched. Actions such as uploading the application package, installing the application in the device, or launching the application are displayed in the Console.

LogCat is another useful tool to debug your application. It is an Android logging system that displays all the log messages generated by the system in the running device. Log messages have several levels of significance: verbose, debug, information, warning, and error.

Finally, you also have **DDMS**, an excellent debugging tool available in the SDK that is available directly in Android Studio. This tool is the main topic of this chapter.

To open the DDMS tool in Android Studio, navigate to **Tools | Android | Monitor (DDMS included)**. Alternatively, you can click on the Android icon present in the toolbar, which will open a window with the DDMS perspective.

Once the perspective is open, as shown in the following screenshot, you can see the list of connected devices to the left-hand side of the screen, along with a list of the processes running on each device. On the right-hand side of the screen, you can see the detailed information of the process. This information is divided into seven tabs: **Threads, Heap, Allocation Tracker, Network Statistics, File Explorer, Emulator Control**, and **System Information**. **LogCat** and **Console** are accessible at the bottom of the window.

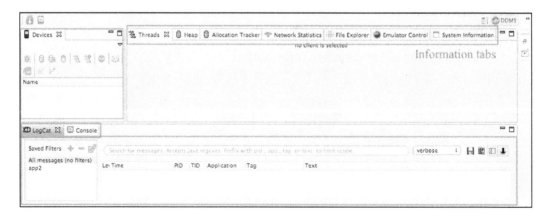

Threads

The **Threads** tab displays the list of threads that are a part of the selected process. Applications have one main thread, also called as the **UI thread**, which dispatches the events to the **user interface** (**UI**) widgets. To perform long operations, it is necessary to create new threads so that the main thread is not blocked. If the main thread gets blocked, the whole UI will also get blocked.

To illustrate the working of this tool, run the following example. In Android Studio, create a new basic project with a main layout and a main activity. Add a button to the main layout named, for example, Start New Thread. Create a new method to be executed when the button is clicked and add the following code in the method:

```
public void startNewThread(View v){
  new Thread(new Runnable() {
    public void run() {
      Thread.currentThread().setName("My example Thread");

      try{
        Thread.sleep(30000);
      } catch (InterruptedException e){
        e.printStackTrace();
      }
    }
  }).start();
}
```

The preceding method creates a new thread in the application, although it does nothing and contains only a sleep instruction. You can set the thread a name to recognize it easily. Run the application and open the DDMS perspective.

Select your application process from the **Devices** section and click on the Update Threads icon present on the toolbar of the Devices section and the threads will be loaded in the content of the tab. The **Status** column indicates the thread state, **utime** indicates the total time spent by the thread executing user code, **stime** indicates the total time spent by the thread executing system code, and **Name** indicates the name of the thread. You can identify the main thread in the result list with the ID number **1**, as shown in the following screenshot:

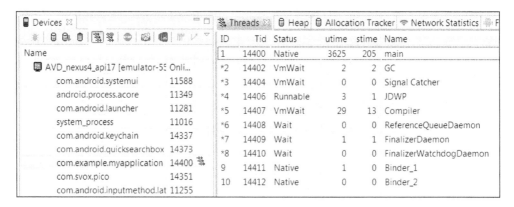

Click on the **Start New Thread** button of your application and notice that a new thread appears in the list as can be observed in the following screenshot, **My example Thread**:

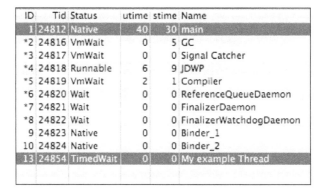

The thread is active for a period of 30 seconds. Every time you click on the **Start New Thread** button, a new thread is created.

This tool is especially useful while creating threads in our application apart from the main thread. Thanks to this tool, we can easily check whether our threads are being executed at a certain point of the execution or whether they are performing as expected in memory usage.

Method profiling

The **method profiling** tool is used to measure the performance of the methods of a selected process. With this tool, you can access the number of calls of a method and the CPU time spent on their execution. There are two types of values available, the exclusive time and the inclusive time:

- **Exclusive time**: This refers to the time spent in the execution of the method itself.

- **Inclusive time**: This refers to the total time spent in the execution of the method, which includes both the time spent by the method as well as the time spent by any other method called inside the method.

To illustrate the working of this tool, we are going to run the following example. Create a new basic project with a main layout and a main activity in Android Studio. You can also reuse the project created in the previous section. Add a button to the main layout, for example, Start Method Hierarchy. Create a new method that is to be executed when the button is clicked and add the following code in the method:

```
public void startMethodHierarchy(View v){
   secondMethod();
}
```

Add the second and the third method in your activity, shown as follows:

```
private void secondMethod() {
   thirdMethod();
}

private void thirdMethod() {
   try{
     Thread.sleep(30000);
   } catch (InterruptedException e){ e.printStackTrace(); }
}
```

As seen in the previous code, you create a hierarchy of method calls that you will be able to observe in the method profiling. To take a look at your method profiling data, select your application process in the devices section and click on the Start Method Profiling icon present on the toolbar of the **Devices** section. Click on the **Start Method Hierarchy** button of your application and wait for a period of at least 30 seconds so that the third method finishes its execution. Once the third method finishes its execution, you can stop the method profiling by clicking on the Stop Method Profiling icon.

When you stop the method profiling, a new tab with the resultant trace will appear within the DDMS perspective. The top of this new tab represents the method calls in a time graph where each row belongs to each thread of the application. The bottom of the trace represents the summary of the time spent on a method in a table.

To search for your application package and main activity, click on the **Name** label to order the methods by their name, for example, `com/example/myapplication/app/ MainActivity`. The three methods (`startMethodHierarchy`, `secondMethod`, and `thirdMethod`) should appear in the list as is shown in the following screenshot:

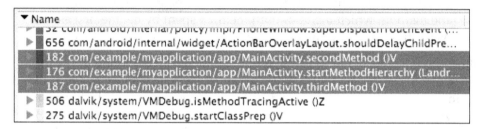

On expanding the detailed information of the `secondMethod`, you can see that the parent is the `startMethodHierarchy` method and that the `thirdMethod` method is its child. This information is presented in the following screenshot:

Name	Incl Real Time	Excl Real Time
182 com/example/myapplication/app/MainActivity.secondMethod ()V	30001,191	0,053
▼Parents		
176 com/example/myapplication/app/MainActivity.startMethodHierarchy...	30001,191	
▼Children		
self	0,053	
187 com/example/myapplication/app/MainActivity.thirdMethod ()V	30001,138	

Also, examine the exclusive and inclusive real times. The preceding screenshot reveals that the inclusive real time for `thirdMethod` was 30001,138 ms, because of the sleep clause of 30 seconds. The time spent in the execution of the `secondMethod` itself is 0,053 ms (exclusive real time), but since the inclusive time includes the time spent by the children methods, its inclusive real time was 30001,191 ms.

Method profiling can be used to detect methods that are spending more time than anticipated in their execution. With this information, you can learn which methods are causing problems and need to be optimized. You can also learn which methods are more time-consuming so that you can avoid unnecessary calls to them.

Heap

The **Heap** tab stores all new objects created in the application. The **garbage collector** (**GC**) deletes the objects that are not referred anymore, releasing unused memory. The **Heap** tab displays the heap usage for a selected process.

To illustrate the working of this tool, run the following example. Create a new basic project with a main layout and a main activity in Android Studio. Add a button to the main layout, for example, Start Memory Consumption. Create a new method to be executed when the button is clicked and add the following code to the method:

```
public void memoryConsumption(View v){
   list = new ArrayList<Button>();
   for (int i = 0; i <= 1000; i++) {
     list.add(new Button(this));
   }
}
```

Finally, add the declaration of the list as a global variable in the activity. This way, you are preventing the GC to release the memory that stores the list after the method finishes its execution. The declaration of the list as a global variable in the activity is shown as follows:

```
private List<Button> list;
```

In this method, you are creating a large number of new objects, for example, a list containing 1000 buttons. Using this method, you are going to examine how the creation of the list is reflected in the heap. Run the application and open the DDMS perspective. Select the application process in the **Devices** tab and click on the Update Heap icon present on the toolbar to enable it. The heap information is shown after a GC execution. Select the **Heap** tab and click on the **Cause GC** button, and you'll see the heap usage.

The first table of the tab displays a summary: the total size, the allocated space, the free space, and the number of allocated objects. The statistics table presents the details of the objects that are allocated on the heap by its type: number of objects, total size of the objects, size of the smallest and largest objects, median size, and average size. We can select each type individually. This action will load the bottom bar graph with the number of objects of that type ordered by its size in bytes. We can then click on the graph using the right button of the mouse to change its properties: title, colors, font, labels, and so on. We can also save it as a PNG image.

Observe the number of data objects allocated on the heap as shown in the following screenshot:

Heap updates will happen after every GC for this client

ID	Heap Size	Allocated	Free	% Used	# Objects
1	2,988 MB	2,731 MB	263,117 KB	91,40%	41.772

Display: Stats

Type	Count	Total Size
free	501	244,305 KB
data object	24.822	763,172 KB
class object	3.118	893,945 KB
1-byte array (byte[], boolean[])	104	194,953 KB
2-byte array (short[], char[])	9.880	665,102 KB
4-byte array (object[], int[], float[])	3.832	277,594 KB
8-byte array (long[], double[])	16	2,117 KB
non-Java object	122	5,484 KB

Click on the **Start Memory Consumption** button of the application. In the DDMS perspective, cause more GC executions and note how the number of objects increases while the method is being executed. The following screenshot shows the heap information when the method has already finished its execution. The allocated data objects have grown from 24.822 to 60.821.

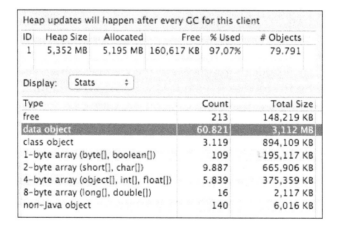

Heap updates will happen after every GC for this client

ID	Heap Size	Allocated	Free	% Used	# Objects
1	5,352 MB	5,195 MB	160,617 KB	97,07%	79.791

Display: Stats

Type	Count	Total Size
free	213	148,219 KB
data object	60.821	3,112 MB
class object	3.119	894,109 KB
1-byte array (byte[], boolean[])	109	195,117 KB
2-byte array (short[], char[])	9.887	665,906 KB
4-byte array (object[], int[], float[])	5.839	375,359 KB
8-byte array (long[], double[])	16	2,117 KB
non-Java object	140	6,016 KB

Finally, you can also try to change the declaration of the list so that it becomes a local variable in the `memoryConsumption` method. Repeat the previous process and note that the new data objects are released by the GC once the execution of the method is finished.

Allocation Tracker

The **Allocation Tracker** tab displays the memory allocations of the selected process. The allocation tracker, unlike the heap tool, shows the specific objects being allocated along with the thread, the method, and the line code that allocated them.

You can again run the previous example created for the heap monitor to show the results of the allocation tracker. Select the application process and in the **Allocation Tracker** tab and click on the **Start Tracking** button to start tracking the memory information. Now, click on the **Get Allocations** button. This will get the list of allocated objects, which includes a filter on the top of the tab that you can use to filter the objects allocated in your own classes.

Click on the **Start Memory Consumption** button of the application. In the DDMS perspective, again click on the **Get Allocations** button and observe the new objects that are listed in the results. The objects are the buttons created in the `memoryConsumption` method.

The results table presents the allocation size, the thread, the object or class, and the method in which each object was allocated. Click on any of the `Button` objects to see more information as shown the following screenshot.

You can notice that the `Button` object is allocated in the main activity in the `memoryConsumption` method, and the line of code that allocated it is the line number 26.

Whenever you need to examine the objects allocated in the heap, you can use the allocation tracker. You can analyze the interactions in your application and improve the memory usage.

The following screenshot shows the details of the `Button` objects:

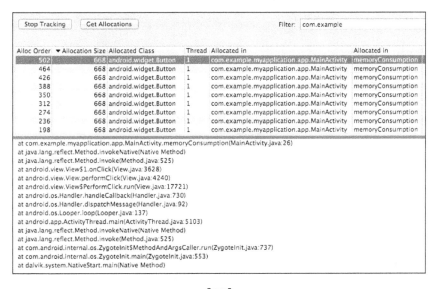

Network Statistics

The **Network Statistics** tab displays the network resources used by our application. Let's create a simple example to test this tool. Create a new project and add the following permissions in your `manifest` file:

```
<uses-permission android:name="android.permission.INTERNET" />
<uses-permission android:name="android.permission.ACCESS_NETWORK_
STATE" />
```

In the main layout, add a button named, for example, `Start Network Connection`. Create a new method to be executed when the button is clicked and add the following code:

```
public void startNetworkConnection(View v){
  new Thread(new Runnable() {
    public void run() {
      try{
        // Small image
        TrafficStats.setThreadStatsTag(0x0001);
        downloadURL("http://goo.gl/iGoYng");
        TrafficStats.clearThreadStatsTag();

        Thread.sleep(5000);

        // Medium image
        TrafficStats.setThreadStatsTag(0x0002);
        downloadURL("http://goo.gl/eQHDRh");
        TrafficStats.clearThreadStatsTag();

        Thread.sleep(5000);

        // Large image
        TrafficStats.setThreadStatsTag(0x0003);
        downloadURL("http://goo.gl/tUDnRv");
        TrafficStats.clearThreadStatsTag();
      } catch (IOException e){
        e.printStackTrace();
      } catch (InterruptedException ie){ ie.printStackTrace(); }
    }
  }).start();
}
```

Using the preceding example, you are downloading three images of different sizes: small, medium, and large. Considering that connecting to the network is a long operation, we need to execute the code in a new thread. Using an `AsyncTask` class is a better solution, but instead the `Thread` class is used to keep the code cleaner. After downloading an image and before downloading the next one, you will have to wait for a period of 5 seconds so that the results displayed later are not confusing. Finally, to clearly separate the different downloads, we establish a different tag for each download using the `setThreadStatsTag` and `clearThreadStatsTag` methods of the `TrafficStats` class. The `TrafficStats` class provides network traffic statistics such as the number of bytes or packages received and transmitted.

To download an image, you have to add the following method in your activity:

```
private Bitmap downloadURL(String image) throws IOException {
  InputStream is = null;

  try {
    URL url = new URL(image);
    HttpURLConnection conn = (HttpURLConnection)
      url.openConnection();
    conn.setRequestMethod("GET");

    conn.connect();
    int response = conn.getResponseCode();
    is = conn.getInputStream();

    // Convert the InputStream into a bitmap
    return BitmapFactory.decodeStream(is);
  } finally {
    if (is != null) {
      is.close();
    }
  }
}
```

In order to have simple code, the previous method does not execute any additional actions on the images. The images are only downloaded.

Run the application and open the DDMS perspective. To get the network statistics of your application, click on the **Start** button in the **Network** tab. Then, click on the **Start Network Connection** button of the application to start downloading the images. The data transfers will appear in the graph as packets are sent or received. The following screenshot shows the results of the network statistics:

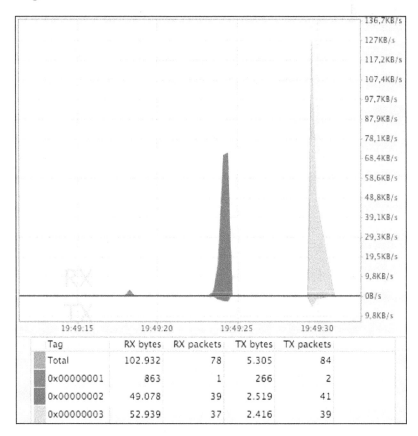

Tag	RX bytes	RX packets	TX bytes	TX packets
Total	102.932	78	5.305	84
0x00000001	863	1	266	2
0x00000002	49.078	39	2.519	41
0x00000003	52.939	37	2.416	39

In the previous screenshot, the download of the three images can be easily identified. The columns **RX bytes** and **RX packets** represent the total number of bytes and packets received. The columns **TX bytes** and **TX packets** represent the total number of bytes and packets transmitted. We can use the network statistics tool to optimize the network requests in our application and control the packets that are being transferred at a certain point of the execution.

File Explorer

The **File Explorer** tab exposes the whole filesystem of the device. We can examine the size, date, or permissions for each element. Navigate to /data/app/yourpackage to search for your application .apk package file. To check the path in which your files are saved when they are created on internal storage, you can use the getFilesDir() method in your activity. The files related to your application are usually located at /data/data/yourpackage. Let's perform an example.

Create a new project and in the main layout add a button named, for example, Create New File. Create a new method to be executed when the button is clicked and add the following code:

```
public void createNewFile(View v){
   String string = "Hello world!";
   FileOutputStream outputStream;

   try {
     outputStream = openFileOutput("MyFile", MODE_PRIVATE);
     outputStream.write(string.getBytes());
     outputStream.close();
   } catch (Exception e) { e.printStackTrace(); }
}
```

Using the previous code, you are creating a new text file on the internal storage of our application. Run the application and open the **File Explorer** tab of the DDMS perspective. Navigate to /data/data/yourpackage/files, which is empty. Click on the **Create New File** button of your application and check that the new file has been created at /data/data/yourpackage/files, as shown in the following screenshot:

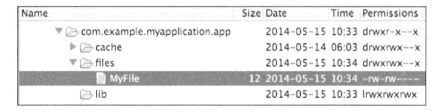

Name	Size	Date	Time	Permissions
▼ 🗁 com.example.myapplication.app		2014-05-15	10:33	drwxr-x--x
▶ 🗁 cache		2014-05-14	06:03	drwxrwx--x
▼ 🗁 files		2014-05-15	10:34	drwxrwx--x
📄 MyFile	12	2014-05-15	10:34	-rw-rw----
🗁 lib		2014-05-15	10:33	lrwxrwxrwx

Emulator Control

The **Emulator Control** tab makes it possible to change states or activities in the virtual device. With this emulator, you can test your application in environments and situations that would otherwise be impossible or time-consuming to achieve. This allows you to check whether it is behaving as expected under the following special conditions:

- **Telephony Status**: You can choose the voice and data status, changing its speed and latency

- **Telephony Actions**: You can simulate an incoming calls, MMS, or SMS

- **Location Controls**: You can change the geolocation of the device

System Information

In the **System Information** tab, you can access **Frame Render Time**, **CPU load**, and **Memory usage** of the device in the form of graphs. You can select your application individually and compare it with the rest of applications that are running on the device.

If you click on the graph with the right button of the mouse, you will see a pop up with the graph properties such as colors, font, and title. The graph can be customized here and can also be saved as a PNG image.

Summary

After going through this chapter, you know how to debug an application. You created several examples in this chapter so you know how to interpret the data provided by the DDMS in each of the tabs available. You now understand better how threads, method calls, memory allocation, and network usage work in Android applications.

In the next chapter, you will apply all that you have learned from this and the previous chapter. You will learn how to identify and mitigate the vulnerabilities in Android applications, and you will be able to create secure applications by following the recommendations included in the next chapter.

4
Mitigating Vulnerabilities

In *Chapter 1, Introduction to Software Security*, we already discussed the most important vulnerabilities that can be exploited in order to compromise your application. Now, you need to learn what measures you can take in order to address these vulnerabilities and make your application more secure. What easy steps can be taken in order to achieve this?

This chapter will show you how to mitigate vulnerabilities. Removing or at least treating vulnerabilities will significantly reduce the risks of your system. We'll begin by learning how to validate input fields. We'll also learn how to avoid code injection, especially the most common one: SQL injection. We'll then see recommended practices when handling user credentials and we will learn how to make our components more secure in order to avoid vulnerabilities in the interapplication communications.

The topics that will be covered in this chapter are as follows:

- Input validation
- Permissions
- Handling users' data and credentials
- Interapplication communication

Input validation

According to the Android development guidelines, the lack of sufficient input validation measures is one of the most common security problems in Android applications. There are several problems that can be derived from insufficient input validation such as buffer overflows, null pointers, off-by-one errors, inconsistencies in the database, and even code injection problems.

Now, we will see some tips that will help us to mitigate this vulnerability.

We can use the `inputType` attribute in order to limit the possible characters the user can set in a field. For example, if we have an `EditText` field where we want a telephone number, we can define the `EditText` as follows in your layout file:

```
<EditText
  android:id="@+id/EditTextTelephone"
  android:hint="@string/telephone"
  android:layout_width="fill_parent"
  android:layout_height="wrap_content"
  android:inputType="phone">
</EditText>
```

Although this should not be considered a security feature, it can help to mitigate this vulnerability. However, in order to ensure that the field is correct, additional measures should be taken.

For example, if we have `EditText` for an e-mail, we can check if its content matches the format of an e-mail simply by using the `Pattern` class from the `java.util.regex` package and the `Pattern` class from the `java.util` package:

```
public void isEmail(EditText et) {
  if (et.getText()== null) return false;
  else return Patterns.EMAIL_ADDRESS.matcher
    (et.getText().toString()).matches();
}
```

There are more patterns available in this class that we can use:

- `DOMAIN_NAME`: This pattern is used to check the domain names
- `EMAIL_ADDRESS`: This pattern is used to check the e-mail addresses
- `IP_ADDRESS`: This pattern is used to check the IP addresses
- `PHONE`: This pattern is intended to check the substrings that are similar to phone numbers in text and should not be used to validate a phone number
- `TOP_LEVEL_DOMAIN`: This pattern is used to check the **Internet Assigned Numbers Authority (IANA)** top-level domains
- `WEB_URL`: This pattern is used to check most parts of the web URLs

If we need to validate an input that is not in this list, we can use our own regular expressions. There are plenty of options to do the validation, but using the `Pattern` class from the `java.util.regex` package is recommended. To learn more about regular expressions, which will allow you to define your own patterns, you can check the official documentation at `http://developer.android.com/reference/java/util/regex/Pattern.html`.

SQL injection

One of the most common and harmful attacks is a particular kind of code injection where unauthorized SQL queries can access or even alter our database. To illustrate this situation, let's consider the following example where you have the following code to check the username and password that was just entered by the user:

```
// We have the username/password in two EditTexts
String username = usernameEditText.getText().toString();
String password = passwordEditText.getText().toString();
// We form our query
String query =
"SELECT * FROM users WHERE username = '" + username + "' AND
password = '" + password +"'";
SQLiteDatabase db = this.getWritableDatabase();
// The method rawQuery performs the query
Cursor c = db.rawQuery(query, null);
// In c you have a cursor to the user if there was a match in the
query
if (c.getCount!=0) return true; // If there is one result, grant
access
```

So what's the problem with the preceding code? An attacker can simply write a username and enter the following string in `EditText` for password:

```
'' OR '1'='1'
```

This will grant the user access to the username since the string query will appear as follows:

```
"SELECT * FROM users WHERE username = 'admin' AND password = '' OR '1'
= '1'"
```

The best defense against this vulnerability is to use parameterized queries. The most important methods that we will be using are as follows:

- `query(Uri uri, String[] projection, String selection, String[] selectionArgs, String sortOrder)`

- `insert(Uri uri, ContentValues)`

- `update(Uri uri, ContentValues values, String selection, String[] selectionArgs)`

- `delete(Uri uri, String selection, String[] selectionArgs)`

Note that if the `selectionArgs` parameter contains any meaningful SQL characters, those characters are sanitized and can therefore mean no harm to the integrity of the database. In order to execute the code used in the previous example safely, we can use the method shown in the following code:

```
// We have the username/password in two EditTexts
String username = usernameEditText.getText().toString();
String password = passwordEditText.getText().toString();
// We set the URI of the table;
String tableName = "USERS";
// We set the projection
String [] projection = new String [] {"username", "password"}
// We set the WHERE clause or selection
String selection = "username=? AND password=?";
// Finally we set the selection arguments
String [] selectionArgs = new String[] {username, password};
// Now we get the database
SQLiteDatabase db = this.getWritableDatabase();
// The method rawQuery performs the query
Cursor c = db.query(tableName, projection, selection, selectionArgs,
null);
// In c you have a cursor to the user if there was a match in the
query
if (c.getCount!=0) return true; // If there is one result, grant
access
```

Permissions

The Android sandboxing system alienates applications from each other. This means that the applications must explicitly share resources through the use of permissions. In order to access the additional capabilities, we need to declare the permissions that we require in our manifest, and these permissions must be accepted by the user after installation.

If our application does not have access to many permissions, it reduces the vulnerabilities that may affect our application. When developing the application, we should always try to request as few permissions as possible. For example, try to store data locally instead of asking for a permission for external storage. If it is not possible, we can obviously request permissions but we should address the vulnerabilities that these permissions can lead to.

If the system-defined permissions are not enough, we can create our own permission to use, which will be defined and will require other entities to ask for permission when required. When creating a permission, we have to consider the different protection levels available:

- `normal`: This is the lowest possible permission level and is set by default
- `dangerous`: This permission level can be granted by the user during installation
- `signature`: This permission level is granted by the system if a requesting app is signed with the same certificate as the app that declared the permission
- `signatureOrSystem`: This permission level is granted by the system if a requesting app is in the Android system image or is signed with the same certificate as the app that declared the permission

Always try to use the `signature` permissions since they are transparent to the user and grant access only to applications signed by the same developer. If we need to use the `dangerous` permission level, we have to understand that this permission is granted by the user and, therefore, needs to be well explained when defined. Users can decide not to install the application if they do not understand the permission that they have to grant or if they perceive it as a possible harm.

We will see some examples of creating permissions in the following sections.

Handling a user's data and credentials

The best way to handle a user's data and credentials is to minimize the use of this information. We should have access to the user data, store user data, or transmit user data only when it is completely necessary.

In the cases where handling user's data and credentials is necessary, there are some considerations that we should have as developers:

- Consider using hash or nonreversible forms of data if the logic of your application allows it.
- Do not expose user's data to other applications on the device. Try to make the interprocess communication as strict as possible. Programming with more flexible interprocess communication permissions can be more comfortable, but it can also be a huge vulnerability in your system.
- Minimize the use of APIs that access sensitive information, especially when the information is personal data. Different APIs have different privacy policies and can even be malicious sometimes.

- Make sure you understand what each and every piece of data that we have to supply to a third-party component is for. When you don't understand why a third-party component or API requires certain data, it is better not provide it.

- Limit the number of times users are asked for credentials as much as possible. Asking for credentials a number of times can make the user less aware of possible phishing attacks.

- Logs are a shared resource in Android, and therefore you should be careful about which information you write onto these logs.

- Avoid transmitting unnecessary information whenever it is possible. When treating sensitive information, evaluate whether it is necessary to transmit that information on the server. If the operation can be performed locally, you should perform it locally.

- When using a username and password authentication system, be sure not to store this information on the device. If it is strictly necessary to do so, use cryptography methods and never store it as plain data.

You can avoid some of these problems using the Android class `AccountManager`. The class `AccountManager` provides access to the user's online accounts that are set in the device. Google, Facebook, and WhatsApp have their own authenticators that are used to manage the authentication of your application. This also has an added value, that is, to avoid the process of registration, which sometimes can drive away lazy users. You will learn more about this authentication method in *Chapter 7, Authentication Methods*.

Interapplication communication

As we seen in *Chapter 2, Security in Android Applications*, there are ways to communicate between Android apps as they cannot share data due to Application sandboxing. This communication raises security challenges that should not be overlooked.

Securing Intents

When using Intents, there are two kinds of vulnerabilities: unauthorized Intent receipt and Intent spoofing. An unauthorized Intent receipt happens while using an implicit Intent. As the Intent is broadcasted, there is no guarantee that the intended recipient will receive it. A malicious application can declare an implicit Intent by declaring all the possible actions in the intent filter. This kind of interception can lead to DoS and phishing attacks.

The best way to protect against this kind of vulnerability is to be very cautious with implicit Intents.

 If you are sharing some private information, avoid using implicit Intents.

When possible, and especially while sharing private information, your application should consider using explicit Intents. You can make the recipient explicit by setting the destination class using the method setClassName (Context ctxt, String className) as follows:

```
Intent i = new Intent();
i.setClassName("com.example.myapplication",
  "com.example.myapplication.MyActivity");
```

You can also use the setPackage (string packageName) method to limit the access to a single package:

```
Intent i = new Intent();
i.setPackage("com.example.myapplication");
```

An application with an exported component that does not expect Intents from a malicious application is vulnerable to Intent spoofing attacks. As a developer, you should limit your component's exposure by setting different permission level requirements in the manifest.

The default values of certain properties can be misleading and may change from one version to another. It is a good idea to indicate the nature of your activity explicitly. For example, let's make our activity PrivateActivity private:

```
<activity
  android:name=".PrivateActivity"
  android:exported="false">
</activity>
```

If we want to make our activity accessible to external applications, we can explicitly indicate which applications have the selective access. In this case, we'll make SelectiveActivity accessible to other applications through our own permission. Then, we can use this permission to indicate selective access to SelectiveActivity using the Intent filter, as shown in the following code:

```
<permission
  android:description="Packt permission"
  android:name="packt.permission"
  android:protectionLevel="signature"/>
```

```
<activity
android:name=".SelectiveActivity"
  android:exported="true"
  android:permission="packt.permission">
  <intent-filter>
    <action android:name="packt.action.NAME_ACTION"/>
  </intent-filter>
</activity>
```

 Intent filters are not a security feature. They perform input validation in your receiver in order to verify the data received.

Securing the content providers

In *Chapter 2, Security in Android Applications* we have learned about the content provider mechanism that allows applications to share raw data. One external component can use an authority name as a handle to perform SQL queries to both read and/or write content. We should be careful and use a content provider only when it is completely necessary and take the following precautions:

- Use separate read and write provider-level permissions. We can specify each of them with the attribute `android:readPermission` and `android:writePermission`. We can also use both the attributes by using `android:permission`.

- Use `path-permission` to specify each URI that you want to control. In this way, you can allow permission for a single or different URIs in your provider.

This mechanism is also vulnerable to SQL injections. In order to easily avoid this vulnerability, Android supports parameterized queries. The content provider methods support parameterization. The methods that are used in parameterized queries to a content provider are the same as to any other SQL database, and we have already seen them in this chapter.

Summary

In this chapter, you learned how to mitigate the most important vulnerabilities that can affect our Android application. You know how to use regular expressions in order to validate an input. You have also learned about SQL injections and how parameterized queries can help overcome this vulnerability. We know how to handle user and critical information. Finally, we learned how to use Intents and content providers in the most secure way possible.

In the next chapter, you will learn how to preserve the privacy of our data. You will learn how to handle the data when stored locally, the different possibilities, and ways to secure them. You will also learn about cryptography and how to encrypt local data.

5
Preserving Data Privacy

Most applications need to save some kind of data. You want to learn how to use the storage options provided by the Android system, how can you protect your data application, what security measures should be taken in each type of storage, and how can you use encryption in Android to preserve the privacy of your data.

This chapter presents the mechanisms offered by Android to preserve user data privacy. You will learn to handle data when it's stored on the device, what are the risks involved with the storage, the different storage options, and how to secure the storage. You will also learn about cryptography and how to encrypt local data.

The topics that will be covered in this chapter are:

- Data privacy
- Encryption
- Using encryption to store data

Data privacy

Data privacy is an important concern for applications because a lot of information is stored and managed in the applications: contacts, e-mails, bank accounts, messages, agenda, social networks, and so on. Some of this information can also be considered as **sensitive data**. Sensitive data can be any of the following types of information:

- Information that allows you to identify a device or the user of that device such as the phone number or the **International Mobile Station Equipment Identity (IMEI)** number of that device
- Information from the resources of the device such as the GPS location of that device

- Information created and managed by the applications
- Users' personal data such as photos or messages

As a developer, your responsibility is to protect the privacy of the information that is stored by your application. There are different mechanisms to store your application data in Android, and each storage mechanism is meant to keep a specific kind of information. The storage mechanisms provided by Android are shared preferences, internal and external storage, and database storage.

Shared preferences

Shared preferences are used to save the collection of key-value pairs of the primitive data types such as `boolean`, `float`, `int`, `long`, and `string`. These key-values pairs are saved in your application data in the form of an XML file, which is stored on the device at `/data/data/yourpackage/shared_prefs/`. If you only need one shared preference file, you can get the default one by using the `getPreferences()` method. If you need to create more than one shared preference file, you can specify its name by using the `getSharedPreferences()` method. Both these methods are received as parameters in the operating mode. The operating mode is `static final int`, which can have the following values:

- `MODE_PRIVATE`: The shared preferences in this mode are private and only your application can work with them
- `MODE_WORLD_READABLE`: The shared preferences in this mode can be read by other applications
- `MODE_WORLD_WRITEABLE`: The shared preferences in this mode can be edited by other applications

To illustrate these three modes, create a new application project and in the `onCreate` method of the main activity, add the following to code to create three shared preference files:

```
SharedPreferences sharedPref = getSharedPreferences("com.example.
MyPrefsFile", MODE_PRIVATE);
SharedPreferences.Editor editor = sharedPref.edit();
editor.putBoolean("KeyA", true);
editor.commit();

SharedPreferences sharedPref2 = getSharedPreferences("com.example.
MyReadablePrefsFile", MODE_WORLD_READABLE);
SharedPreferences.Editor editor2 = sharedPref2.edit();
editor2.putBoolean("KeyB", true);
editor2.commit();
```

```
SharedPreferences sharedPref3 = getSharedPreferences("com.example.
MyWriteablePrefsFile", MODE_WORLD_WRITEABLE);
SharedPreferences.Editor editor3 = sharedPref3.edit();
editor3.putBoolean("KeyC", true);
editor3.commit();
```

The private shared preference file is named `MyPrefsFile`, the readable shared preference file is named `MyReadablePrefsFile`, and the writeable shared preference file is named `MyWriteablePrefsFile`. In each file, we save a Boolean value. Execute the application and open the DDMS perspective. Open the **File Explorer** tab and navigate to your application files under `/data/data/yourpackage/`. You'll see that a new `shared_prefs` folder has been created and inside this folder the three preference files have also been created, as shown in the following screenshot:

Name	Size	Date	Time	Permissions
▼ 📂 shared_prefs		2014-05-27	14:02	drwxrwx--x
📄 MyPrefsFile.xml	111	2014-05-27	14:02	-rw-rw----
📄 MyReadablePrefsFile.xml	111	2014-05-27	14:02	-rw-rw-r--
📄 MyWriteablePrefsFile.xml	111	2014-05-27	14:02	-rw-rw--w-

Observe the system permissions of the three preference files. The `MyReadablePrefsFile` file allows any user of the system to read it and the `MyWriteablePrefsFile` file allows any user of the system to write it. Creating a shared preference file using any of these two modes is very dangerous as the privacy of the data stored in them is not preserved. There are better mechanisms than shared preferences to distribute data between applications such as the content providers.

 Always create your shared preferences using the private mode to reduce security holes.

The mode flag of the shared preferences determines only the system permission of the file. The XML file is not encrypted. You can check this by downloading the `MyPrefsFile` file from the DDMS perspective. Open the file using any text editor and notice that the saved data is not encrypted and can be read. The content of the downloaded shared preference file is as shown in the following code:

```
<?xml version='1.0' encoding='utf-8' standalone='yes' ?>
<map>
    <boolean name="KeyA" value="true" />
</map>
```

The actual user, any application with the root system permission, or any attacker that gains access to the device is able to read this file.

 Do not save sensitive data on shared preferences as they are stored in an unencrypted file.

Files in the internal storage

Internal storage allows you to save any type of file in your application's data directory, which is stored on the device at /data/data/yourpackage/files/. To create a file, you can use the openFileOutput() method in which you can specify the mode flag as a parameter. The mode flag can have the following values:

- MODE_PRIVATE: The file is private in this mode flag and only your application can work with it.

- MODE_APPEND: In this mode flag, if the file already exists, data is written to the end of the existing file. If the file does not exist, the system permissions for the file are like the permissions for MODE_PRIVATE.

- MODE_WORLD_READABLE: The file in this mode flag can be read by other applications.

- MODE_WORLD_WRITEABLE: The file in this mode flag can be edited by other applications.

Just like the shared preferences, creating a file using the MODE_WORLD_READABLE or MODE_WORLD_WRITEABLE flag is very dangerous as the privacy of the file content is not preserved. In fact, both the flags were deprecated in Android API Level 17.

 Do not use the flags MODE_WORLD_READABLE or MODE_WORLD_ WRITEABLE to create your files.

The created files are not encrypted, therefore you can encrypt the file content to preserve its privacy.

Files in the external storage

External storage refers to a world-readable part of storage in an Android device. We tend to think about external storage as an SD card, but actually, external storage can also be a non-removable storage. External storage may not always be available, for example, if the SD card is removed in case the storage was provided by an SD card, or if the storage has been mounted to a PC. For this reason, you must always check external storage state before using it, using the following code:

```
String exStorageState = Environment.getExternalStorageState();
```

In the external storage, there are two types of files: **public** and **private**. These two terms should not be confused with the file permissions. The public and private files in external storage are discussed in detail as follows:

- **Public files**: These files in the external storage are files that can be shared with other applications, such as pictures, music, or ringtones. To fetch the path of the directories in which these types of files should be stored, you can use the `Environment.getExternalStoragePublicDirectory()` method. You indicate the type of the public content you want to work with as a parameter. Some examples for this type flag are `DIRECTORY_PICTURES`, `DIRECTORY_ALARMS`, `DIRECTORY_DOCUMENTS`, `DIRECTORY_MUSIC`, and `DIRECTORY_RINGTONES`.

- **Private files**: These files on the external storage are files that belong to your application and hence, they have no utility outside your application. These files are removed when your application is uninstalled. Remember that although these types of files belong to your application, their permissions are still world readable. To get the path of your private directory, you can use the `context.getExternalFilesDir()` method.

 Do not save sensitive information on external storage because files in it are globally readable and writeable.

The database storage

SQLite databases allow you to store your data in a private database. The database is a `.db` file, which is created in the internal storage directory of your application. The specific path for this file is `/data/data/yourpackage/databases/`. Databases are private but not encrypted and thus, the user or any attacker that gains access to the device can read the database content.

Sensitive data should be encrypted and very sensitive data should not be saved on the device.

Encryption

Encryption is the process of encoding data into a form that cannot be understood by unauthorized users. Sensitive data stored in the device should be encrypted to preserve its security. You can encode data to save it as shared preferences, as files in the internal storage, in databases, or even in external storage. But you should remember that sensitive data must not be stored on external storage. There are two types of encryption methods:

- **Symmetric**: In symmetric encryption, the keys for encoding and decoding are the same. Some examples of well-known symmetric algorithms are DES, Triple DES, AES, Serpent, Twofish, and Blowfish.

- **Asymmetric or public-key**: In asymmetric or public-key encryption, the key for encoding is different from the key for decoding. The encryption key can be public and hence, anyone can encode data using the public key. But only the owner of the private key is able to decode it. Some examples of well-known asymmetric algorithms are RSA, Diffie-Hellman, ElGamal, and DSA.

Using a symmetric algorithm is enough to encrypt our data since nobody else needs the public encryption key. The following figure explains how symmetric encryption works:

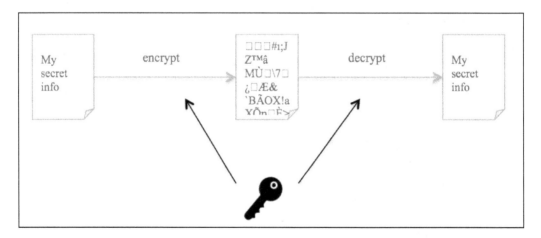

Let's see an example of how to encrypt some information. The class that provides implementations for encryption and decryption is the `Cipher` class from the `javax.crypto` package. To use this class, you need to create an instance indicating the encryption algorithm and optionally the mode or the padding. You can see both examples in the following code snippets:

```
Cipher c = Cipher.getInstance("AES");
Cipher c = Cipher.getInstance("AES/CBC/PKCS5Padding");
```

The next step is to initialize the instance using the `init` method of the `Cipher` class. This method receives the operation—encrypt or decrypt—and the key to use for the encryption, as shown in the following code snippets:

```
c.init(Cipher.ENCRYPT_MODE, key);
c.init(Cipher.DECRYPT_MODE, key);
```

To perform the operation, use the `doFinal` method, as shown in the following code snippet:

```
byte[] finalBytes = c.doFinal(initialBytes);
```

Both methods—`init` and `doFinal`—admit more parameters that can be consulted in the Android reference at `http://developer.android.com/reference/javax/crypto/Cipher.html`.

The encryption methods

The following code shows the complete method to encrypt a text using the encryption methods discussed in the preceding section:

```
public byte[] encrypt(String text, Key key)
throws NoSuchPaddingException, NoSuchAlgorithmException,
InvalidKeyException, BadPaddingException, IllegalBlockSizeException
{
    Cipher c = Cipher.getInstance("AES/CBC/PKCS5Padding");
    c.init(Cipher.ENCRYPT_MODE, key);
    byte[] encodedBytes = c.doFinal(text.getBytes());

    return encodedBytes;
}
```

The following code shows the complete method to decrypt a text using the decryption methods discussed in the preceding section:

```
public String decrypt(byte[] text, Key key)
throws NoSuchPaddingException, NoSuchAlgorithmException,
InvalidKeyException, BadPaddingException, IllegalBlockSizeException
{
  Cipher c = Cipher.getInstance("AES/CBC/PKCS5Padding");
  c.init(Cipher.DECRYPT_MODE, key);
  byte[] decodedBytes = c.doFinal(text);

  return new String(decodedBytes);
}
```

Generating a key

To generate a key in order to encrypt or decrypt your data, you can just write down your own key as a `String` data type. For example, you can use the following line of code but with a different key:

```
private final String key = "123456789012345678901234567890012";
```

To obtain a `Key` object so that it can be passed as a parameter to your encryption and decryption methods, you can use the `SecretKeySpec` class. The simplest constructor of this class receives the key bytes and algorithm name, as shown in the following line of code:

```
SecretKeySpec sks = new SecretKeySpec(key.getBytes(), "AES");
```

Although writing your own key is simple, keeping it visible in your code is not secure. Any attacker that gains access to your code can get the key. The right way to generate your key is by using the `SecureRandom` and `KeyGenerator` classes. The objective is to obfuscate the key.

The `SecureRandom` class, as specified in the Android reference, generates cryptographically secure pseudorandom numbers. Using the default constructor is recommended so that an instance of the strongest provider is returned. Setting a seed may also be insecure because it may replace the strong default seed. The `KeyGenerator` class generates symmetric cryptographic keys. You should remember to save the generated keys so that you can use them later, even when the application is closed and restarted.

You should invoke the `SecureRandom` class using the default constructor and without setting any seed.

The following code shows the complete method to generate a key for both encryption and decryption:

```
public SecretKeySpec generateKey() throws NoSuchAlgorithmException
{
  SecureRandom secureRandom = new SecureRandom();
  KeyGenerator keyGenerator = KeyGenerator.getInstance("AES");
  keyGenerator.init(256, secureRandom);
  SecretKeySpec sks = new SecretKeySpec(key.getEncoded(), "AES");
  return sks;
}
```

Using encryption to store data

Using all the methods discussed in the earlier sections, you can now encrypt any information in your application, as shown in the following code:

```
String myData = "My secret information";

SecretKeySpec sks = generateKey();
byte[] encoded = encrypt(myData, sks);
String decoded = decrypt(encoded, sks);

Log.d("MAIN - Encoded: ",
Base64.encodeToString(encoded, Base64.DEFAULT));
Log.d("MAIN - Decoded: ", decoded);
```

The results generated in LogCat are shown in the following screenshot:

Application	Tag	Text
com.examp...	MAIN - Original:	My secret information
com.examp...	MAIN - Encoded:	GnCNTM+3b1KFl7P0MGYvWUSHwoUMIovpixa9AmjH1VI=
com.examp...	MAIN - Decoded:	My secret information

The previous example can be adapted to encrypt the content of a file on the internal storage of your application, as shown in the following code:

```
String myData = "My secret information in my internal file";
SecretKeySpec sks = generateKey();
byte[] encoded = encrypt(myData, sks);

FileOutputStream fos =
openFileOutput("MyEncryptedFile.txt", Context.MODE_PRIVATE);
fos.write(encoded);
fos.close();
```

On executing the code in your main activity, the `MyEncryptedFile.txt` file will be created in the internal storage, as seen in the following screenshot. Download the file and open it in any text editor. Notice that the content is not understandable because it is encoded.

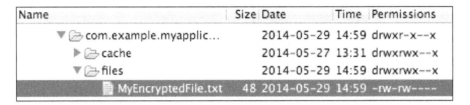

Name	Size	Date	Time	Permissions
▼ 🗁 com.example.myapplic…		2014-05-29	14:59	drwxr-x--x
▶ 🗁 cache		2014-05-27	13:31	drwxrwx--x
▼ 🗁 files		2014-05-29	14:59	drwxrwx--x
📄 MyEncryptedFile.txt	48	2014-05-29	14:59	-rw-rw----

It is mandatory for you to store the persistent data encrypted retaining the key that has been used for encoding. The key cannot be saved in the internal storage as it is considered to be sensitive data. In Android 4.3, the `KeyStore` facility was provided but `KeyStore` only stores public or private keys. Symmetric keys cannot be stored in `KeyStore`. To provide additional protection, the key should not be directly accessible to the application.

 The key used to encrypt your data should be kept in a safe place. If you lose the key, the data cannot be decoded.

The best solution to keep your key safe is to send it to your server so that the key is never allocated in the device itself. The user or any attacker that gains physical access to the device cannot obtain the key. In *Chapter 6, Securing Communications*, you will learn how to protect your external communications.

An alternative solution is to generate the key from a password that the user has to introduce when starting his/her application. The key is therefore not stored in the device and is remembered by the user. This solution is very secure but it requires the user to introduce a password every time the application is started, affecting the usability of your application. In *Chapter 7, Authentication Methods*, you will learn more about the authentication methods. To generate a key from a password, you can use the **PBKDF2** algorithm implemented in the `SecretKeyFactory` class, as shown in the following code snippet:

```
SecretKeyFactory skf = SecretKeyFactory.getInstance("PBKDF2WithHmacS
HA1");
```

The key is generated creating a PBEKeySpec object, which receives the password, a byte array as salt, the iteration count of the algorithm, and the derived key length. The method to generate a key of this type is as shown in the following code:

```
private static byte[] salt = "3r4ghe69".getBytes();

public SecretKeySpec generatePassKey(String password)
throws NoSuchAlgorithmException, InvalidKeySpecException {
  KeySpec keySpec =
  new PBEKeySpec(password.toCharArray(), salt, 500, 256);

  SecretKeyFactory skf = SecretKeyFactory.getInstance("PBKDF2WithHmac
SHA1");

  SecretKey key = skf.generateSecret(keySpec);
  SecretKeySpec sks = new SecretKeySpec(key.getEncoded(), "AES");
  return sks;
}
```

The salt byte array can also be stored in the internal storage.

Summary

In this chapter, you learned more about the different types of storage for our data application in Android. You also learned about the characteristics and risks of each type of storage. You also know how to encrypt the user data and manage the local storage. You have created the necessary methods to encrypt your sensitive data and use it in your application.

In the next chapter, you will learn how to preserve the privacy of your data when it is sent or received over a network from an internal or external device. You will also learn how to secure the network using protocols such as HTTPS.

6
Securing Communications

This chapter presents the mechanisms offered by Android to secure communications between an Android application and an external entity. By the end of this chapter, you will know how to secure connections. You will see some implementations through code examples using Android Studio.

Most applications need to share some sort of data. You should learn how to protect this data especially when sensitive information such as personal data or authentication information is being transferred.

The topics that will be covered in this chapter are:

- HTTPS
- SSL and TSL
- Server and client certificates
- Android Studio
- Code examples using HTTPS

HTTPS

Hypertext Transfer Protocol Secure (HTTPS) is considered an application layer protocol based on HTTP. It is designed to transfer the hypertext data securely. HTTPS is largely used by bank entities, online shops, and in general, any online service that requires sending protected data.

First of all, you need to understand what HTTPS being an application layer protocol means. There are two important conceptual models that standardize the internal functions of a communication system. These models are the **Open Systems Interconnection (OSI)** model and the **Transmission Control Protocol/Internet protocol suite (TCP/IP)** model. The OSI model consists of seven abstraction layers while the TCP/IP model is simplified into only five layers. Each layer does not represent a protocol but a level in which a protocol is encapsulated. For simplicity and as its use is more common, we will focus on the TCP/IP model, discussed as follows:

- **The physical layer**: This layer defines the most basic form of communication — the electrical and physical specifications. The connection is defined between two directly connected elements over a physically established communication medium (cable, air, and so on.). The IEEE 802.11 specifications over which Wi-Fi, Bluetooth, and even USB work are some examples of the protocols that operate in the physical layer.

- **The link layer**: This layer defines the communication established between two elements that are in the same local network. Notice that there might be several physical elements (routers, switches, and furthermore) between these two elements. The **Media Access Control (MAC)** protocols, such as Ethernet, ISDN, or DSL work in this layer.

- **The internet layer**: This layer is responsible for establishing communication between two elements across multiple networks. There are two main functions carried out in this layer: host identification and packet routing. The most known example of a protocol working in this layer is IP, with IPv4 and IPv6 being the most extended versions of IP.

- **The transport layer**: This layer defines the communication between two processes in different hosts that can potentially be several networks apart. This layer uses ports for the purpose of providing communication channels needed by the applications. The most common protocols that work on the transport layer are TCP and UDP. While TCP is connection-oriented and is in charge of identifying lost packages and resending them, UDP is connectionless and does not perform these checks.

- **The application layer**: This is the layer that applications use in order to provide user services. This layer is the most important for developers, since it is usually the one we will be working with. The model of this layer enables you to treat the transport layer and lower layers as a black box; they provide a service and you do not need to worry about them. There are hundreds of protocols that work over the application layer, for example HTTP and its secure version HTTPS, **File Transfer Protocol (FTP)**, **Simple Mail Transfer Protocol (SMTP)**, and so on. The application layer in the TCP/IP model can be compared to a combination of the application layer, presentation layer, and session layer in the OSI model, as shown in the following figure:

OSI Model	TCP/IP Model
Application Layer	Application Layer
Presentation Layer	
Session Layer	
Transport Layer	Transport Layer
Network Layer	Internet Layer
Data Link Layer	Link Layer
Physical Layer	Physical Layer

HTTPS is considered to be an application layer protocol that uses cryptographic methods based on **Secure Sockets Layer (SSL)** or his elder brother **Transport Layer Security (TLS)** to ensure the security of sensitive hypertext data. However, technically, it is not a protocol itself but the result of combining HTTP in the application layer with SSL or TLS in the transport layer. The security is therefore not provided in the application layer but in the transport layer. HTTPS also specifies that the transport layer should use the TCP protocol to ensure that every package is received correctly, as shown in the following figure:

Application Layer	HTTPS
Transport Layer	SSL/TLS
	TCP
Network Layer	IP

Although HTTPS is based on the application layer protocol HTTP, there are some differences between the two of them. The most important are:

- URLs start with http:// when using the HTTP protocol and with https:// when using the HTTPS protocol

- By default, HTTP uses the TCP port 80. On the other hand, HTTPS uses port 443 by default

- HTTP is vulnerable to man-in-the-middle attacks and eavesdropping, and is designed to solve these vulnerabilities and minimize the risks

If you want to learn more about the differences between HTTP and HTTPS, you can use a packet analyzer to see how the exchange of hypertext is performed with each protocol, as shown in the following screenshot. To do this, we recommend **Wireshark** (http://www.wireshark.org/), a free and **open source software** (OSS). You will learn more about this tool in *Chapter 10, Supporting Tools*.

Time	Source	Destination	Protocol	Length	Info
015662000	192.168.1.7	91.198.174.202	TCP	78	51983 > https [SYN] Seq=0 Win=65535 Len=0 MSS=1460 WS=16 TSval=600
015752000	192.168.1.7	91.198.174.202	TCP	78	51984 > https [SYN] Seq=0 Win=65535 Len=0 MSS=1460 WS=16 TSval=600
015841000	192.168.1.7	91.198.174.202	TCP	78	51985 > https [SYN] Seq=0 Win=65535 Len=0 MSS=1460 WS=16 TSval=600
016121000	192.168.1.7	91.198.174.208	TCP	78	51986 > https [SYN] Seq=0 Win=65535 Len=0 MSS=1460 WS=16 TSval=600
016207000	192.168.1.7	91.198.174.208	TCP	78	51987 > https [SYN] Seq=0 Win=65535 Len=0 MSS=1460 WS=16 TSval=600
016273000	192.168.1.7	91.198.174.208	TCP	78	51988 > https [SYN] Seq=0 Win=65535 Len=0 MSS=1460 WS=16 TSval=600
016334000	192.168.1.7	91.198.174.208	TCP	78	51989 > https [SYN] Seq=0 Win=65535 Len=0 MSS=1460 WS=16 TSval=600
016396000	192.168.1.7	91.198.174.208	TCP	78	51990 > https [SYN] Seq=0 Win=65535 Len=0 MSS=1460 WS=16 TSval=600
077811000	91.198.174.192	192.168.1.7	TCP	74	https > 51981 [SYN, ACK] Seq=0 Ack=1 Win=14480 Len=0 MSS=1452 SACK
077912000	192.168.1.7	91.198.174.192	TCP	66	51981 > https [ACK] Seq=1 Ack=1 Win=132480 Len=0 TSval=600190552
078144000	192.168.1.7	91.198.174.192	TLSv1.2	583	Client Hello
082017000	91.198.174.202	192.168.1.7	TCP	74	https > 51982 [SYN, ACK] Seq=0 Ack=1 Win=14480 Len=0 MSS=1452 SACK
082089000	192.168.1.7	91.198.174.202	TCP	66	51982 > https [ACK] Seq=1 Ack=1 Win=132480 Len=0 TSval=600190556

```
▷ Frame 231: 78 bytes on wire (624 bits), 78 bytes captured (624 bits) on interface 0
▽ Ethernet II, Src: Apple_1a:f2:1a (b8:e8:56:1a:f2:1a), Dst: CameoCom_27:03:7c (18:17:25:27:03:7c)

0000  18 17 25 27 03 7c b8 e8  56 1a f2 1a 08 00 45 00   ..%'.|.. V.....E.
0010  00 40 32 d6 40 00 40 06  3b 9c c0 a8 01 07 5b c6   .@2.@.@. ;.....[.
0020  ae d0 cb 17 01 bb bc 0d  c8 e4 00 00 00 00 b0 02   ........ ........
0030  ff ff c7 11 00 00 02 04  05 b4 01 03 03 04 01 01   ........ ........
0040  08 0a 23 c6 2e 1b 00 00  00 00 04 02 00 00         ..#..... ......
```

SSL and TLS

SSL is a cryptographic protocol that supports secure connections over a network. SSL was originally designed by Netscape. There are three main versions of SSL and being the latest one, SSL 3.0 is the most commonly used over the Internet. SSL 3.0 is supported by 99.5 percent of the websites on the Internet.

TLS is an update of SSL 3.0. It is compatible with SSL 3.0 but it weakens the security level. The most extended version of TLS is TLS 1.0 although there are two updates: TLS 1.1 and TLS 1.2. TLS 1.0 is supported by 99.3 percent of the websites on the Internet.

An SSL or TSL connection is always initiated by the client. Data transferred under the SSL protocol is encrypted using a symmetrical algorithm like **Data Encryption Standard** (**DES**). An asymmetrical algorithm is used to exchange the keys for the symmetrical algorithm. The basic steps to establish an SSL connection are as follows:

1. **Client -> server**: The client initiates the communication with the server sending a "Hello" message. This message contains different cryptographic options available to the client sorted by preference of use.

2. **Server -> client**: The server responds by sending a Hello message. In this case, the message contains the cryptographic method and the compression method chosen.

3. **Server -> client**: The server sends their digital certificate. The standard is to use an X.509 certificate. If the server requires a certificate from the client, a Certificate Request message is sent.

4. **Client -> server**: The client cross-checks the certificate received from the server with a list of known authorities. If the authority is not recognized, the client can ask the user for permission to manually accept the certificate. The client also assesses if the connection parameters are adequate. If everything is acceptable, the client generates a symmetric random key, which is cyphered with the server public key received in step 3. The cyphered symmetric key is then sent to the server.

5. **Client -> server**: The server receives the encrypted symmetric key and proceeds to decrypt it using his private key.

6. **Client <-> server**: Now both the client and the server know the symmetric key and can start a secure connection.

Server and client certificates

In this section, you will learn more about how certificates are used and generated. A certificate is a digitally signed statement from an authority that grants a certain value to the public key of the subject. They are used in asymmetric encryption methods.

X.509 certificate is a standard format and must have the following information:

- **Version**: This is the X.509 version number
- **Serial number**: This is the sequence number of the certificate
- **Signature algorithm**: This is the identifier of the algorithm used to sign the certificate
- **Issuer**: This is the name of the authority that signs the certificate
- **Validity**: This is the period of time during which the certificate should be considered valid
- **Subject**: This is the name of the subject of the public key
- **Subject public key**: This is the public key itself and its related information

You will now learn how to create a self-signed X.509 certificate with no additional installation necessary whatsoever. You will see two easy ways to generate a certificate: using a tool available in every **Java Development Kit (JDK)** called Keytool from the terminal and using the same tool from Android Studio in a more visual way. There are many other options to create certificates like the OpenSSL client.

Keytool in the terminal

Open your operating system terminal or go to **Tools | Open Terminal** in Android Studio, and write the following command:

```
keytool -genkey -keyalg RSA -alias selfsigned -keystore my_keystore.jks
-storepass password -validity 360 -keysize 2048
```

The parameter -genkey is the action the tool and is going to perform. In this case, it will generate a key. The parameter -keyalg specifies the algorithm to be used; in this case, we want to use RSA. The parameter -alias is for the name or alias of the keys being generated. The parameter -keystore indicates which JKS file is going to be used to store the keys. The parameter -storepass indicates the master password used to access the JKS file. If the file is being created just like the one created in this example, you can set the password, but if the keystore already exists, you should introduce its password. The parameter -validity specifies the number of days the certificate is valid. Finally, with the parameter -keysize, you can indicate the size of the key in bits. In this example, the parameter -keysize has a value of 2048 because we have used an RSA algorithm whose keys are normally between 1024 and 2048 bits.

The execution of the previous command will prompt a sequence of questions. Make sure that when asked for your first name and last name, you answer with the domain name of the server you want to get the certificate from. If you have problems executing this, you can add the keytool to the path of the system. The application is available in the /bin folder of your JDK installation folder and can also be executed directly from there:

```
What is your first and last name?
  [Unknown]:  www.mydomain.com
What is the name of your organizational unit?
  [Unknown]:  My Application
What is the name of your organization?
  [Unknown]:  My Company
What is the name of your City or Locality?
  [Unknown]:  Murcia
What is the name of your State or Province?
  [Unknown]:  Murcia
What is the two-letter country code for this unit?
  [Unknown]:  ES
```

```
Is <CN=www.mydomain.com, OU=My Application, O=My Company, L=Murcia,
ST=Murcia, C=ES> correct?
  [no]:  y
Enter key password for <my_keystore>
        (RETURN if same as keystore password):
```

This process will generate a `my_keystore.jks` file in a JKS format. This file contains both private key and public key certificates so make sure not to share it as your private key is what should be kept from other entities. In order to extract the certificate, you can execute the following command:

```
keytool -export -alias selfsigned -file certificate.crt -keystore my_
keystore.jks -storepass password
```

This will generate a file called `certificate.crt`, which contains the certificate. Using the very same tool, we can print its contents using the following command:

```
keytool -printcert -file certificate.crt
```

This will print the information of our self-signed certificate:

```
Owner: CN=www.mydomain.com, OU=My Application, O=My Company, L=Murcia,
ST=Murcia, C=ES

Issuer: CN=www.mydomain.com, OU=My Application, O=My Company, L=Murcia,
ST=Murcia, C=ES

Serial number: 71e760d8

Valid from: Tue Jun 03 17:42:47 BST 2014 until: Fri May 29 17:42:47 BST
2015

Certificate fingerprints:
   MD5:  63:34:55:9F:11:74:3A:02:EB:D3:8F:E2:7B:A3:1B:25

   SHA1:  CA:CF:6E:75:83:F9:01:D9:13:45:A5:DE:D2:95:EB:2E:31:BA:2D:B4

   SHA256:  5A:A8:68:87:3D:89:B2:26:60:0F:55:DB:68:F1:24:6E:81:33:8B:3B:B2:
57:07:36:D4:06:B2:1A:C3:03:DE:F0

Algorithm: SHA256withRSA

Version: 3
```

You can see how `Owner` and `Issuer` are the same since the certificate is self-signed. If it was signed by a different CA, `Issuer` would be that CA.

Android Studio

Android Studio has a tool to sign your APK. This option internally makes use of keytool to create a certificate with which the APK is later signed. You can use the first step of this process to generate your certificate. Navigate to **Build | Generate Signed APK**. A wizard will appear asking you to select an already existing certificate or create a new one. Click on **Create New** and the following window will appear:

As you can see, it asks for the exact same information we filled in using the keytool. You can follow the same instructions as in the previous section to fill the information required in this form.

If you want to learn more about certificates and certificate authorities, you can check the section on *App Signing* in the Android development documentation since the signature of apps also uses the certificates and certificate authorities at http://developer.android.com/tools/publishing/app-signing.html.

Code examples using HTTPS

You already understand how HTTPS works theoretically, but how can an Android developer use secure connections using HTTPS?

To establish an HTTP connection, all you need to do is run the following three lines of code:

```
URL url = new URL("http://wikipedia.org");
HttpURLConnection connection = (HttpURLConnection) url.
openConnection();
InputStream in = connection.getInputStream();
```

Wikipedia supports secure communications, so let's change the code to make it use HTTPS instead of HTTP, as shown in the following code:

```
URL url = new URL("https://wikipedia.org");
HttpsURLConnection connection = (HttpsURLConnection) url.
openConnection();
InputStream in = connection.getInputStream();
```

Can you see the difference? Well, if you can see the difference, congratulations! You have a very sharp eye. If you can't, here is a little hint: check the protocol in the URL again and the HttpURLConnection class. Now you see the little **s** after **http** in the URL and in the class name, and yes, that is all you need to do to start a secure communication with a server that supports HTTPS.

Easy right? Well, that is not entirely true. You may work with certificates that are signed by a trusted **Certificate Authority (CA)** or you may not work with certificates signed by a trusted CA. There are three different cases where this can happen:

- The CA that issued the certificate is unknown
- The certificate was self-signed
- The server is missing an intermediate CA

If the issuer of the certificate is an unknown CA, an SSLHandshakException will occur. If you know this is going to happen, you can create HttpsURLConnection, which trusts certain CAs that are not in the list of the system-trusted CAs. The class TrustManager is used by the system in order to validate unknown certificates. In the following example, we will create KeyStore, which contains our trusted CAs. With KeyStore, we will initiate TrustManager, which trusts the CAs included in KeyStore. With TrustManager created, we will initiate an SSL connection, shown as follows:

```
// First we read the certificate from a file
CertificateFactory cf = CertificateFactory.getInstance("X.509");
InputStream certificate = new BufferedInputStream(new
FileInputStream("my_keystore.jks"));
Certificate ca = cf.generateCertificate(certificate);

// Now we create the KeyStore containing the certificate
String type = KeyStore.getDefaultType();
KeyStore keyStore = KeyStore.getInstance(type);
keyStore.load(null, null);
keyStore.setCertificateEntry("CA", ca);

// Now we can initiate the TrustManager with our KeyStore
String algorithm = TrustManagerFactory.getDefaultAlgorithm();
TrustManagerFactory tmf = TrustManagerFactory.getInstance(algorithm);
tmf.init(keyStore);

// With the TrustManager we initiate a SSLContext
SSLContext context = SSLContext.getInstance("TLS");
context.init(null, tmf.getTrustManagers(), null);

// Now we can initiate the connection using the SSLContext
URL url = new URL("https://www.mydomain.com");
HttpsURLConnection connection = (HttpsURLConnection) url.
openConnection();
connection.setSSLSocketFactory(context.getSocketFactory());
InputStream in = urlConnection.getInputStream();
```

As you can see, the last four lines of the code are similar to what we were doing before worrying about the certificate authorities. We have removed some try clauses for the sake of clean code, but if you copy the code to Android Studio, just follow its suggestions to treat exceptions.

In this example, we used the certificate that we generated using the Java tool—keytool. If you remember, the certificate we generated was self-signed, which is the second case and not the first. From a coding perspective, both situations are similar. In the first one, CA is not recognized so we create TrustManager in order to acknowledge it. In the second case, it is exactly the same, but the issuer of the certificate is also the subject.

If the server is missing an intermediate CA, there will also be an `SSLHandshakeException` since there is a missing CA in the trust chain. There are two ways you can solve this situation:

- **From the server side**: You can reconfigure the server to include the missing CA in the trust chain. This is obviously possible only if you administrate the server.

- **From the client side**: The only problem you have is that there is a missing CA, therefore, that CA is an unknown CA. You can therefore use the class `TrustManager` as we did in the first two cases to trust the missing CA directly.

Summary

In this chapter, you learned about network communications in your Android application. Now you understand how the most common protocols to secure connections work. You also learned how to use the APIs that Android offers to secure your application's communications. Finally, you learned about certificate generation.

In the next chapter, you will learn about authentication methods. You will see how two-key and three-key authentication methods work. You will also learn about using biometric authentication in your application.

7
Authentication Methods

This chapter presents different types of authentication methods used in Android mobile devices. This chapter will help readers choose the proper authentication method for their mobile application.

First, you will learn about multifactor authentication and the different authentication factors, such as the knowledge factor, the possession factor, and the inherence factor. You will then learn how to make your own implementation of a login system for your Android application. You will also learn about authenticating different services using AccountManager.

The topics that will be covered in this chapter are:

- Multifactor authentication
- Login implementations
- AccountManager

Multifactor authentication

If you think of an authentication method, the first method that will come to your mind will always be the combination of a username and a password. While its simplicity makes it one of the most extended authentication methods in all kinds of software, it is not the safest method. The **multifactor authentication** approach combines a set of authentication methods. Access is granted only if each method derives a positive result. **Two-factor** authentication and **three-factor** authentication involve two and three authentication factors, respectively. Although two-factor authentication and above are often considered to be strong authentication methods and are in fact more secure, you can also achieve strong authentication for your service using only one authentication factor. There are three kinds of authentication factors that serve as a taxonomy for authentication techniques: the knowledge factor, the possession factor, and the inherence factor.

The knowledge factor

The combination of a username and password is an example of a knowledge factor. When using a knowledge factor, the user is required to provide information he/she knows in order to grant access: *something the user knows*.

The most widely used methods are:

- **Username/password**: The combination of a certain kind of identifier for the user, generally a username or an e-mail address, and a password is the most extended authentication technique. While the username or e-mail address may be public, the password should always remain a secret.

- **Pattern**: Patterns are used as authentication methods since the human brain is more likely to remember graphical patterns than strings of characters or numbers. There are several types of patterns that often involve a 3 x 3 grid although bigger grids are also used.

- **PIN**: The PIN is a very basic password that has been traditionally used in the banking system for ATMs, credit cards, and so on. It consists of an array of digits. It is technically an implementation of the password techniques, where only digits are allowed.

The pattern and PIN techniques are available by default as the access control to your Android system, as shown in the following screenshot:

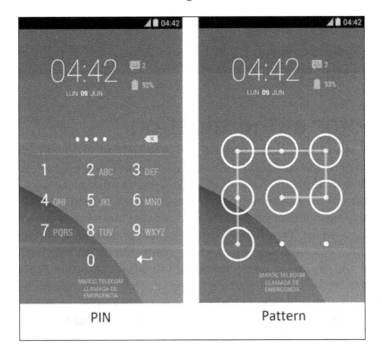

The possession factor

The most basic and well-known example of a possession factor is a key that opens a door. In order to authenticate a user trying to access a resource, they are required to provide a physical object they possess: *something the user has*.

There are several examples of possession factors. The most typical techniques based on a possession factor are physical tokens such as smartcards or magnetic cards. The technique most commonly used in Android is probably the **cryptographic keys**. We already learned about cryptographic keys in the earlier chapters, and although these keys are digital and the user does not have material access to them, they are considered as *something the user possesses*. There are other algorithms like **Time-based One-Time Password** (**TOTP**). TOTP consists of combining a secret key with the current timestamp to generate a password that is temporarily valid.

The inherence factor

The inherence factor is based on *something the user is*. The techniques based on this factor are the ones that are used frequently, but the ones with the brightest future. **Biometric authentication** measures the distinctive characteristics of individuals to identify the user.

There are two types of biometric identifiers:

- **Physiological characteristics**: This is when the shape of the body is measured. The most commonly known examples are the fingerprint analysis, face recognition, and iris or retina recognition. In Android, there are several implementations of face recognition, and some smartphones come with a hardware support for fingerprint scan like the HTC One Max.
- **Behavioral characteristics**: This is when the behavior of a person is measured. Physiological characteristics are more consolidated than behavioral characteristics. The most extended behavioral characteristic is voice recognition. There are different implementations of voice recognition for Android.

Login implementations

We will now see a small example on how to perform authentication using Android. The example we are going to see here uses the login and password combination technique. We are going to start with a very simple example and increase the functionalities as well as the complexities in every iteration.

First of all, we will define EditText and Button, shown as follows:

```
<EditText
    android:id="@+id/etUsername"
    android:layout_width="wrap_content"
    android:layout_height="wrap_content"/>
<EditText
    android:id="@+id/etPassword"
    android:layout_width="wrap_content"
    android:layout_height="wrap_content"
    android:inputType="textPassword"/>
<Button
    android:id="@+id/bLogin"
    android:layout_width="wrap_content"
    android:layout_height="wrap_content"
    android:onClick="login"
    android:text="Login"/>
```

Now, we are going to check whether the combination of a username and password is good or not. To start, we will simply check whether both the username and password are admin, shown as follows:

```
EditText username = (EditText)findViewById(R.id.etUsername);
EditText password = (EditText)findViewById(R.id.etPassword);

String sUsername = username.getText().toString();
String sPassword = password.getText().toString();

if (sUsername.equals("admin") && sPassword.equals("admin")) {
  // Grant access
} else {
  Toast.makeText(getApplicationContext(), "Wrong password",
    Toast.LENGTH_SHORT).show();
}
```

This is obviously not a good example of a secure authentication method but from the example, we can learn some useful things. For example, the inputType parameter of EditText can be set to textPassword when using a password field.

You are normally going to make a request to your server in order to authenticate the user. For example, in this case, we use `SimpleHTTPClient` to make the request, shown as follows:

```
EditText username = (EditText)findViewById(R.id.etUsername);
EditText password = (EditText)findViewById(R.id.etPassword);

String sUsername = username.getText().toString();
String sPassword = password.getText().toString();

ArrayList<NameValuePair> params = new ArrayList<NameValuePair>();
params.add(new BasicNameValuePair("username", sUsername);
params.add(new BasicNameValuePair("password", sPassword);
String response = SimpleHttpClient.executeHttpPost(
  "http://www.mydomain.com/login",
  params);
// Analyze response with what the server is supposed to answer
```

You have to realize that this implementation also has big problems, even bigger than the previous one. In this case, the username and password are being transferred online and any attacker could see them in plain text. In order to avoid this, we can use an HTTPS connection as we have seen in the previous chapter.

There are some login implementations that hash the username and password before sending them to the server in order to increase the security, for example, using the SHA1 hash shown as follows:

```
EditText username = (EditText)findViewById(R.id.editText1);
EditText password = (EditText)findViewById(R.id.editText2);

String sUsername = SHA1.Sha1Hash(username.getText().toString());
String sPassword = SHA1.Sha1Hash(password.getText().toString());

ArrayList<NameValuePair> params = new ArrayList<NameValuePair>();
params.add(new BasicNameValuePair("username", sUsername);
params.add(new BasicNameValuePair("password", sPassword);

String response = SimpleHttpClient.executeHttpPost(
  "http://www.mydomain.com/login",
  params);
// Analyze response with what the server is supposed to answer
```

The problem with this implementation is that the hashed username and password can still be sniffed by an attacker as they are still being transferred in plain text. This is a common mistake. So when you store passwords, you want to make sure you store their hashed versions. The correct solution would be to send the password using a secure connection. Later, when you want to check if the password is right, you apply the hash function to the password provided by the user and compare it to the stored hashed password to see whether they match.

In *Chapter 6, Securing Communications*, we saw how to establish an HTTPS connection between your application and a server. You can use that information and the preceding example to create a secure login implementation for your application.

AccountManager

The `AccountManager` class provides access to all the registered users' online accounts. This way, the user only needs to provide his/her credentials once for each account and then he/she can grant access to these applications in a simpler way. Using the `AccountManager` class, you can get a token that can be used as a form of authentication in different services.

The steps that you need to take in order to make use of this feature are as follows:

1. First, you need to modify the `manifest` file and add permission to use credentials:

   ```
   <uses-permission
     android:name="android.permission.USE_CREDENTIALS">
   </uses-permission>
   ```

2. Once your application can use credentials, you can get an instance of `AccountManager` using the `get(Context c)` method:

   ```
   AccountManager am = AccountManager.get(this);
   ```

3. Now, you have an instance of `AccountManager`, but you need to know which accounts are available. To do this, you can use the `getAccountsByType(String s)` method. The `String` parameter is the name of the account type. In this case, we will look for the Facebook accounts:

   ```
   Account [] accounts = am.getAccountsByType("com.facebook.auth.
   login");
   ```

4. You can also use `null` as the parameter to obtain all the available accounts:

   ```
   Account [] accounts = am.getAccountsByType(null);
   ```

5. The getAccountsByName method should also be called if the application is using a previously saved account selection in order to make sure that this account still exists in the device. You can check this by looking up the account in the array of accounts returned by getAccountsByName.

6. Once you have a list of the available accounts, you should ask the user which account is to be used. When the selection is done, you can call the method, shown as follows:

   ```
   getAuthToken(Account account, String authTokenType, Bundle
   options, Activity activity, AccountManagerCallback<Bundle>
   callback, Handler handler).
   ```

7. You will get an authentication token in the AccountManagerFuture<Bundle> object for a particular account, which will automatically prompt the user for acceptance if it is required.

8. In case the token request returns an error, there could be a cached instance of an authentication token that may be being used. You can call the invalidateAuthToken(String accountType, String authToken) method to remove an obsolete token. Once the obsolete token is removed, you can again request a new token using the getAuthToken method.

Summary

In this chapter, you learned about multifactor authentication and the different techniques available in each authentication factor. You also learned how to make your own implementation of a simple login system. Finally, you learned how you can get authentication tokens to access different services by using AccountManager.

In the next chapter, you will learn how to start testing your application, test your user interface, and use the test environment in Android Studio.

8
Testing Your Application

You have learned how to create secure applications. Now, you want to ensure the quality of your Android application. What elements can be tested in Android? How test cases are developed? Does Android Studio support testing?

This chapter introduces the ways of testing an application in Android. In Android, we can design tests to evaluate the **user interface** (**UI**), activities, services, and content providers. In this chapter, we will learn about UI testing.

The topics that will be covered in the chapter are as follows:

- Testing in Android
- The uiautomator API
- The uiautomatorviewer tool
- The UI test project
- Running UI test cases

Testing in Android

The security and quality of Android applications are the key factors to its success. Testing helps you discover bugs and errors in your application, measure its accuracy, and also improve security.

Android testing is based on **JUnit**. JUnit is a framework to write repeatable tests in Java. It evaluates whether the class that is to be tested is working as expected. There are two types of tests to be created in an Android application:

- **Tests that can run on the Java Virtual Machine (JVM)**: If you want to test standard Java classes that do not call the Android API, you can use plain JUnit tests. The execution of this type of test is faster because it does not require any time for deployment on an Android device, especially when running on an emulator.

- **Tests that require the Android SDK**: If you need to evaluate classes that use Android API, tests have to be run on an Android device using the Android JUnit extensions. From now on, we will be using this kind of test since we want to learn how to check Android classes such as activities or the UI components.

Tests are implemented in methods contained in test classes. These tests are organized in test packages. By convention, the test package name is the same as your application package suffixed with `.test`. Test class names are the same as the element to be tested suffixed with `Test`. For example, the test class that evaluates your `MainActivity` file should be named `MainActivityTest`. Test method names are prefixed with `test`. Some examples of method names are `testLayout()` and `testOnClick()`.

Testing the UI

The UI can be evaluated using the white-box testing or black-box testing. In the white-box testing, UI components are checked in the activities that manage them. Activity testing will be explained in the next chapter, that is, *Chapter 9, Unit and Functional Tests*. The black-box testing is based on the `uiautomator` API. This API includes classes to capture and manipulate components in the application under test. This type of test does not require you to know the internal implementation of the application.

Android Studio does not directly support the uiautomator framework, but since it is available in the Android SDK, we can use it anyway. The steps to complete the testing process are as follows:

1. Install the application under test on a device (real device or an emulator).

2. Analyze the UI components of the application under test, employing the uiautomatorviewer tool.

3. Create a Java test project to implement your test cases using the uiautomator API.

4. Compile the test project into a JAR file and install it on the device.

5. Run the implemented tests.

We are going to proceed with a complete UI testing example in the successive sections, but first let's learn about the uiautomator API.

The uiautomator API

The uiautomator API is included in the `uiautomator.jar` library, which can be found in your Android SDK installation folder, under the `<android-sdk>/platforms/` directory. The API includes a TestCase class that extends the JUnit TestCase class: `UiAutomatorTestCase`. To manipulate the UI components, the `UiDevice`, `UiSelector`, `UiObject`, `UiCollection`, and `UiScrollable` classes are also supplied to the API.

The UiDevice class

The `UiDevice` class represents the device. We can get the `UiDevice` instance by calling the `getUiDevice()` method. With this instance object, you can check properties such as the orientation or the display size. You can also perform device-level actions such as clicking on the Home button or taking a screenshot. Some examples of the available methods are as follows:

- `click(int x, int y)`: This method performs a click at the specified coordinates

- `getDisplaySizeDp()`: This method returns the display size in device-independent pixels

- `pressBack()`: This method simulates a press on the back button

- `pressHome()`: This method simulates a press on the home button

- `sleep()`: This method simulates a press on the power button to set the screen off

- `takeScreenshot(File storepath)`: This method takes a screenshot of the current screen

- `wakeUp()`: This method simulates a press on the power button to set the screen on

The UiSelector class

The UiSelector class represents the search criteria to query any UI element on the screen. If no component is found, UiAutomatorObjectNotFoundException is thrown. If more than one component is found, the first one in the layout hierarchy is returned. The UiSelector class offers methods to refine the search. Some of the methods are as follows:

- checked(boolean val): This method matches elements that are checked.

- childSelector(UiSelector selector): This method adds a child selector criteria to the current selector.

- className(String className): This method matches elements of the specified class. For example, you can search for buttons using the following code:

```
new UiSelector().className("android.widget.Button")
```

- resourceID(String id): This method matches the element with the specified ID.

- text(String text): This method matches elements containing the indicated visible text. For example, you can refine the previous search for buttons by adding a second filter, as shown in the following code:

```
new UiSelector().className("android.widget.Button")
.text("Continue")
```

The UiObject class

The UiObject class represents a UI element. The UiObject instances are obtained from the UiSelector instances. The class UiObject provides methods to perform actions on the UI elements. Some examples of the methods are as follows:

- click(): This method performs a click at the center of the UI element

- exists(): This method checks whether the element exists

- getText(): This method returns the text of the element

- isChecked(): This method returns whether the element is currently checked or not

- setText(String text): This method sets the text whether the element allows it (whether it's an editable field)

The UiCollection class

The UiCollection class represents a collection of items. The UiCollection instances are obtained from the UiSelector instances that return a container of other child UI elements. The methods provided by this class are all related to the selection of children, shown as follows:

- getChildByDescription(UiSelector childPattern,String text): This method searches for a child by its description and returns a UiObject object
- getChildByInstance(UiSelector childPattern, int instance): This method searches for a child by its instance number and returns a UiObject object
- getChildByText(UiSelector childPattern, String text): This method searches for a child by its visible text and returns a UiObject object
- getChildCount(UiSelector childPattern): This method returns the child count

The UiScrollable class

The UiScrollable class represents a scrollable collection of items. This class is useful to simulate scrolling and brings hidden elements into view. The UiScrollable instances are obtained from the UiSelector instances. This class presents methods similar to the methods of the UiCollection class and also provides methods to simulate scrolling:

- scrollBackward(): This method performs a backward scroll
- scrollForward(): This method performs a forward scroll
- scrollToBeginning(): This method scrolls to the beginning
- scrollToEnd(): This method scrolls to the end

The uiautomatorviewer tool

The uiautomatorviewer tool serves to take a snapshot of the current screen on an Android device that is connected to the development machine. The snapshot allows you to examine the layout components that are included in the screen. You can learn about how they are structured and their properties such as IDs, texts, classes, and furthermore. The uiautomatorviewer tool is included in the tools directory of the Android SDK installation: <android-sdk>/tools/.

Let's look at an example to show how this tool works. Since we are performing black-box testing, the uiautomatorviewer tool can be applied to any application although it is not developed by us, nor do we have its source code. We are going to use the default Android clock application by following this procedure:

1. Open Android Studio and launch an **Android Virtual Device (AVD)** in the emulator. You can also use a real device connected to your computer.

2. When the device is completely loaded, open the application drawer and select the **Clock** application.

3. Back in the Android Studio IDE, click on the **Tools** menu and select the **Open Terminal** option to open the terminal panel.

4. Using the terminal, navigate to the Android tools folder where the uiautomatorviewer executable is found. In Unix-based systems, you can find it by using the command:

   ```
   $ cd androidSDK/tools/
   ```

5. Launch uiautomatorviewer by using the command:

   ```
   $ ./uiautomatorviewer
   ```

6. The uiautomatorviewer tool is now open and shows an empty window. Click on the button icon from the top bar, which hints at the Device Screenshot (uiautomator dump). This button is marked in red in the following screenshot. This option will take a snapshot of the clock application that is being displayed in the foreground in the emulator.

In the uiautomator viewer, we can inspect the layout elements of the screen. The following screenshot shows the uiautomator viewer after capturing the screen from the clock application. On the left side of the viewer, the snapshot is displayed. You can hover the mouse over it to navigate and select the UI components. On the top-right part of the viewer, the layout hierarchy is listed. We can expand and collapse the layouts and select individual elements. In the following screenshot of our example, the layout containing the hour is selected. On the bottom-right part of the viewer, the properties of the selected component are detailed.

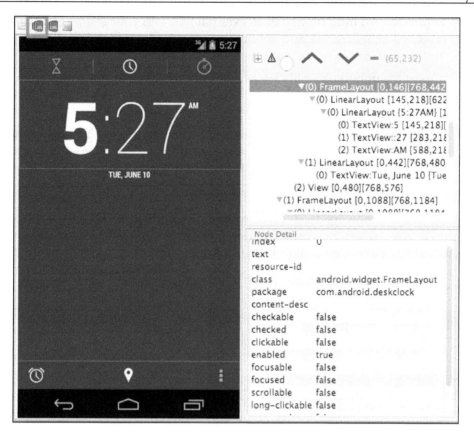

The UI test project

The test code to evaluate the UI of an application has to be included in a normal Java project. This Java project will be built into a JAR file, which will be copied in the Android device to evaluate the application under test. Since Android Studio does not support the uiautomator framework, for this section you can use any other tool that allows you create a Java project. The required steps are as follows:

1. Create a standard Java project. This is the test project where the test code will be implemented using the uiautomator API. You can call this project `UITestProject`.

2. Import the JUnit library into your test project. Currently, JUnit 3.8 is the supported version.

3. Import the Android library as an external JAR into your test project. This JAR is named `android.jar` and is stored in your Android SDK installation folder under `<android-sdk>/platforms/<sdk>/`.

4. Import the uiautomator library as an external JAR into your test project. This JAR is named `uiautomator.jar` and is stored in your Android SDK installation folder under `<android-sdk>/platforms/<sdk>/`.

5. Create a new class in the source folder of your test project. You can name the class `ClockTest.java`. This class is used to implement your test case and therefore, has to extend the `UiAutomatorTestCase` class.

6. Add your test code in the `ClockTest` class.

Your UI test code is now ready. For our example, let's add some simple code just to demonstrate how UI testing works. Create a test method named `testOpenAlarms` to evaluate the alarm button in the clock application. To perform a click on the alarm button, we need to indicate its ID, which can be extracted from uiautomatorviewer, as shown in the following screenshot:

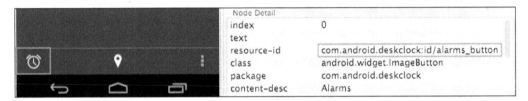

The `resourceId` method of the `UiSelector` class can be used to find the UI component whose ID is `com.android.deskclock:id/alarms_button`. The object created can be checked and if everything is fine, a click is simulated on it:

```
public class ClockTest extends UiAutomatorTestCase {

  public void testOpenAlarms() throws UiObjectNotFoundException {

    UiObject alarmButton = new UiObject(new UiSelector().
    resourceId("com.android.deskclock:id/alarms_button"));

    if(alarmButton.exists() && alarmButton.isEnabled()) {
      alarmButton.click();
    }
  }
}
```

Running UI test cases

The Java test project created in the previous section has to be compiled into a JAR file to run your test cases. The JAR file has to be copied onto the same Android device in which the application under test is running. Follow the next steps to run your test case:

1. Open the terminal panel in Android Studio (**Tools | Open Terminal**).

2. Navigate to the Android Studios `tools` folder where the android executable is found:

   ```
   $ cd androidSDK/tools/
   ```

3. Get the ID of the Android target that you want to use in your project. Execute the android executable with the list of the target actions. This command will list the available Android targets along with their IDs:

   ```
   $ ./android list targets
   ```

4. Execute the `android` executable with the `create uitest-project` action. This command receives the name of the output project (`-n`), the ID of the Android target (`-t`), and the path of your Java test project (`-p`) as parameters. This step is to generate the project's build file as a test project:

   ```
   $ ./android create uitest-project -n UITest -t 1
   -p /Users/myUser/workspace/UITestProject
   ```

    The UI test projects can only target API 16 and above; otherwise, an error will be prompted.

   As a result, the `UITestProject/build.xml` file is generated and the `/Users/myUser/workspace/UITestProject/build.xml` file is added.

5. Build the JAR file from the project using the `build.xml` file obtained before.

6. Copy the JAR file into the device using the `adb` utility:

   ```
   $ cd androidSDK/platform-tools/
   $ ./adb push
     /Users/myUser/workspace/UITestProject/bin/UITest.jar
     /data/local/tmp
   ```

7. Finally, execute the next command to run the UI test case on the connected device:

   ```
   $ ./adb shell uiautomator runtest UITest.jar
     -c com.example.ClockTest
   ```

If you observe the device while the UI test is being executed, you will see how the actions implemented in the testOpenAlarms test method are simulated. The results are shown in the terminal panel as you can see in the following screenshot, in which the test case execution has been successful:

```
Terminal
$ ./adb shell uiautomator runtest UiTest.jar -c com.example.ClockTest
INSTRUMENTATION_STATUS: current=1
INSTRUMENTATION_STATUS: id=UiAutomatorTestRunner
INSTRUMENTATION_STATUS: class=com.example.ClockTest
INSTRUMENTATION_STATUS: stream=
com.example.ClockTest:
INSTRUMENTATION_STATUS: numtests=1
INSTRUMENTATION_STATUS: test=testClock
INSTRUMENTATION_STATUS_CODE: 1
INSTRUMENTATION_STATUS: current=1
INSTRUMENTATION_STATUS: id=UiAutomatorTestRunner
INSTRUMENTATION_STATUS: class=com.example.ClockTest
INSTRUMENTATION_STATUS: stream=.
INSTRUMENTATION_STATUS: numtests=1
INSTRUMENTATION_STATUS: test=testClock
INSTRUMENTATION_STATUS_CODE: 0
INSTRUMENTATION_STATUS: stream=
Test results for WatcherResultPrinter=.
Time: 2.951

OK (1 test)
```

Summary

In this chapter, you learned about testing in Android. You developed black-box testing for your user interface. You also learned how to create a test case for your application UI and how you can run it on a device.

In the next chapter, you will learn more about testing in Android. You will develop test cases to evaluate the activities of your application. You will use unit and functional tests and set up the testing environment using Android Studio.

9
Unit and Functional Tests

You already learned about Android testing in the previous chapter. You know how to develop a black-box test of the UI of your application. Now you want to learn how to implement the white-box testing for your application. Are there different types of activity testing? Does Android Studio support activity testing? How can you get the results of your test cases? We will be covering these points in this chapter.

In this chapter, you will learn how to use unit tests that allow developers to quickly verify the state and behavior of an activity on its own. The chapter will also cover functional tests; their main purpose is to check the interaction between components.

The topics that will be covered in this chapter are as follows:

- Differences between unit and functional tests
- Android testing API
- Creating a simple unit test case
- Creating a simple functional test
- Getting the test results

Testing activities

There are two possible modes of testing activities:

- **Functional testing**: In functional testing, the activity being tested is created using the system infrastructure. The test code can communicate with the Android system, send events to the UI, or launch another activity.
- **Unit testing**: In unit testing, the activity being tested is created with minimal connection to the system infrastructure. The activity is tested in isolation.

In this chapter, we will explore the Android testing API to learn about the classes and methods that will help you test the activities of your application.

The test case classes

The Android testing API is based on JUnit. Android JUnit extensions are included in the `android.test` package. The following figure presents the main classes that are involved when testing activities:

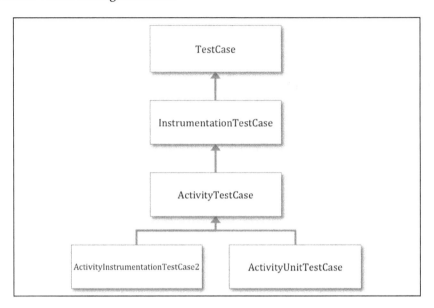

Let's learn more about these classes:

- `TestCase`: This JUnit class belongs to the `junit.framework`. The `TestCase` package represents a general test case. This class is extended by the Android API.

- `InstrumentationTestCase`: This class and its subclasses belong to the `android.test` package. It represents a test case that has access to instrumentation.

- `ActivityTestCase`: This class is used to test activities, but for more useful classes, you should use one of its subclasses instead of the main class.

- `ActivityInstrumentationTestCase2`: This class provides functional testing of an activity and is parameterized with the activity under test. For example, to evaluate your `MainActivity`, you have to create a test class named `MainActivityTest` that extends the `ActivityInstrumentationTestCase2` class, shown as follows:

```
public class MainActivityTest
extends ActivityInstrumentationTestCase2<MainActivity>
```

- `ActivityUnitTestCase`: This class provides unit testing of an activity and is parameterized with the activity under test. For example, to evaluate your `MainActivity`, you can create a test class named `MainActivityUnitTest` that extends the `ActivityUnitTestCase` class, shown as follows:

  ```
  public class MainActivityUnitTest
  extends ActivityUnitTestCase<MainActivity>
  ```

There is a new term that has emerged from the previous classes called `Instrumentation`.

Instrumentation

The execution of an application is ruled by the life cycle, which is determined by the Android system. For example, the life cycle of an activity is controlled by the invocation of some methods: `onCreate()`, `onResume()`, `onDestroy()`, and so on. These methods are called by the Android system and your code cannot invoke them, except while testing. The mechanism to allow your test code to invoke callback methods is known as Android instrumentation.

Android instrumentation is a set of methods to control a component independent of its normal lifecycle. To invoke the callback methods from your test code, you have to use the classes that are instrumented. For example, to start the activity under test, you can use the `getActivity()` method that returns the activity instance. For each test method invocation, the activity will not be created until the first time this method is called. Instrumentation is necessary to test activities considering the lifecycle of an activity is based on the callback methods. These callback methods include the UI events as well.

From an instrumented test case, you can use the `getInstrumentation()` method to get access to an `Instrumentation` object. This class provides methods related to the system interaction with the application. The complete documentation about this class can be found at: `http://developer.android.com/reference/android/app/Instrumentation.html`. Some of the most important methods are as follows:

- **The addMonitor method**: This method adds a monitor to get information about a particular type of Intent and can be used to look for the creation of an activity. A monitor can be created indicating `IntentFilter` or displaying the name of the activity to the monitor. Optionally, the monitor can block the activity start to return its canned result. You can use the following call definitions to add a monitor:

  ```
  ActivityMonitor addMonitor (IntentFilter filter, ActivityResult
      result, boolean block).
  ActivityMonitor addMonitor (String cls, ActivityResult result,
      boolean block).
  ```

The following line is an example line code to add a monitor:

```
Instrumentation.ActivityMonitor monitor =
  getInstrumentation().addMonitor(
  SecondActivity.class.getName(), null, false);
```

- **The activity lifecycle methods**: The methods to call the activity lifecycle methods are: `callActivityOnCreate`, `callActivityOnDestroy`, `callActivityOnPause`, `callActivityOnRestart`, `callActivityOnResume`, `callActivityOnStart`, `finish`, and so on. For example, you can pause an activity using the following line code:

```
getInstrumentation().callActivityOnPause(mActivity);
```

- **The getTargetContext method**: This method returns the context for the application.

- **The startActivitySync method:** This method starts a new activity and waits for it to begin running. The function returns when the new activity has gone through the full initialization after the call to its `onCreate` method.

- **The waitForIdleSync method**: This method waits for the application to be idle synchronously.

The test case methods

JUnit's `TestCase` class provides the following protected methods that can be overridden by the subclasses:

- `setUp()`: This method is used to initialize the fixture state of the test case. It is executed before every test method is run. If you override this method, the first line of code will call the superclass. A standard `setUp` method should follow the given code definition:

```
@Override
protected void setUp() throws Exception {
  super.setUp();
  // Initialize the fixture state
}
```

- `tearDown()`: This method is used to tear down the fixture state of the test case. You should use this method to release resources. It is executed after running every test method. If you override this method, the last line of the code will call the superclass, shown as follows:

```
@Override
protected void tearDown() throws Exception {
  // Tear down the fixture state
  super.tearDown();
}
```

The fixture state is usually implemented as a group of member variables but it can also consist of database or network connections. If you open or init connections in the setUp method, they should be closed or released in the tearDown method. When testing activities in Android, you have to initialize the activity under test in the setUp method. This can be done with the getActivity() method.

The Assert class and method

JUnit's TestCase class extends the Assert class, which provides a set of assert methods to check for certain conditions. When an assert method fails, AssertionFailedException is thrown. The test runner will handle the multiple assertion exceptions to present the testing results. Optionally, you can specify the error message that will be shown if the assert fails. You can read the Android reference of the TestCase class to examine all the available methods at http://developer.android.com/reference/junit/framework/Assert.html. The assertion methods provided by the Assert superclass are as follows:

- assertEquals: This method checks whether the two values provided are equal. It receives the actual and expected value that is to be compared with each other. This method is overloaded to support values of different types, such as short, String, char, int, byte, boolean, float, double, long, or Object. For example, the following assertion method throws an exception since both values are not equal:

  ```
  assertEquals(true, false);
  ```

- assertTrue or assertFalse: These methods check whether the given Boolean condition is true or false.

- assertNull or assertNotNull: These methods check whether an object is null or not.

- assertSame or assertNotSame: These methods check whether two objects refer to the same object or not.

- fail: This method fails a test. It can be used to make sure that a part of code is never reached, for example, if you want to test that a method throws an exception when it receives a wrong value, as shown in the following code snippet:

  ```
  try{
    dontAcceptNullValuesMethod(null);
    fail("No exception was thrown");
  } catch (NullPointerExceptionn e) {
    // OK
  }
  ```

The Android testing API, which extends JUnit, provides additional and more powerful assertion classes: `ViewAsserts` and `MoreAsserts`.

The ViewAsserts class

The assertion methods offered by JUnit's `Assert` class are not enough if you want to test some special Android objects such as the ones related to the UI. The `ViewAsserts` class implements more sophisticated methods related to the Android views, that is, for the `View` objects. The whole list with all the assertion methods can be explored in the Android reference about this class at `http://developer.android.com/reference/android/test/ViewAsserts.html`. Some of them are described as follows:

- `assertBottomAligned` or `assertLeftAligned` or `assertRightAligned` or `assertTopAligned(View first, View second)`: These methods check that the two specified `View` objects are bottom, left, right, or top aligned, respectively

- `assertGroupContains` or `assertGroupNotContains(ViewGroup parent, View child)`: These methods check whether the specified `ViewGroup` object contains the specified child `View`

- `assertHasScreenCoordinates(View origin, View view, int x, int y)`: This method checks that the specified `View` object has a particular position on the origin screen

- `assertHorizontalCenterAligned` or `assertVerticalCenterAligned(View reference View view)`: These methods check that the specified `View` object is horizontally or vertically aligned with respect to the reference view

- `assertOffScreenAbove` or `assertOffScreenBelow(View origin, View view)`: These methods check that the specified `View` object is above or below the visible screen

- `assertOnScreen(View origin, View view)`: This method checks that the specified `View` object is loaded on the screen even if it is not visible

The MoreAsserts class

The Android API extends some of the basic assertion methods from the `Assert` class to present some additional methods. Some of the methods included in the `MoreAsserts` class are:

- `assertContainsRegex(String expectedRegex, String actual)`: This method checks that the expected **regular expression (regex)** contains the actual given string

---

- `assertContentsInAnyOrder(Iterable<?> actual, Object… expected)`: This method checks that the iterable object contains the given objects and in any order

- `assertContentsInOrder(Iterable<?> actual, Object… expected)`: This method checks that the iterable object contains the given objects, but in the same order

- `assertEmpty`: This method checks if a collection is empty

- `assertEquals`: This method extends the `assertEquals` method from JUnit to cover collections: the `Set` objects, `int` arrays, `String` arrays, `Object` arrays, and so on

- `assertMatchesRegex(String expectedRegex, String actual)`: This method checks whether the expected regex matches the given actual string exactly

Opposite methods such as `assertNotContainsRegex`, `assertNotEmpty`, `assertNotEquals`, and `assertNotMatchesRegex` are included as well. All these methods are overloaded to optionally include a custom error message. The Android reference about the `MoreAsserts` class can be inspected to learn more about these assert methods at `http://developer.android.com/reference/android/test/MoreAsserts.html`.

UI testing and TouchUtils

The test code is executed in two different threads as the application under test, although, both the threads run in the same process. When testing the UI of an application, UI objects can be referenced from the test code, but you cannot change their properties or send events. There are two strategies to invoke methods that should run in the UI thread:

- `Activity.runOnUiThread()`: This method creates a `Runnable` object in the UI thread in which you can add the code in the `run()` method. For example, if you want to request the focus of a UI component:

```
public void testComponent() {
  mActivity.runOnUiThread(
    new Runnable() {
      public void run() {
        mComponent.requestFocus();
      }
    }
  );
  ...
}
```

- @UiThreadTest: This annotation affects the whole method because it is executed on the UI thread. Considering the annotation refers to an entire method, statements that do not interact with the UI are not allowed in it. For example, consider the previous example using this annotation, shown as follows:

```
@UiThreadTest
public void testComponent () {
  mComponent.requestFocus();
  ...
}
```

There is also a helper class that provides methods to perform touch interactions on the view of your application: TouchUtils. The touch events are sent to the UI thread safely from the test thread; therefore, the methods of the TouchUtils class should not be invoked in the UI thread. Some of the methods provided by this helper class are as follows:

- **The clickView method**: This method simulates a click on the center of a view

- **The drag, dragQuarterScreenDown, dragViewBy, dragViewTo, dragViewToTop methods**: These methods simulate a click on an UI element and then drag it accordingly

- **The longClickView method**: This method simulates a long press click on the center of a view

- **The scrollToTop or scrollToBottom methods**: These methods scroll a ViewGroup to the top or bottom

The mock object classes

The Android testing API provides some classes to create mock system objects. Mock objects are fake objects that simulate the behavior of real objects but are totally controlled by the test. They allow isolation of tests from the rest of the system. Mock objects can, for example, simulate a part of the system that has not been implemented yet, or a part that is not practical to be tested.

In Android, the following mock classes can be found: MockApplication, MockContext, MockContentProvider, MockCursor, MockDialogInterface, MockPackageManager, MockResources, and MockContentResolver. These classes are under the android.test.mock package. The methods of these objects are nonfunctional and throw an exception if they are called. You have to override the methods that you want to use.

Creating an activity test

In this section, we will create an example application so that we can learn how to implement the test cases to evaluate it. Some of the methods presented in the previous section will be put into practice. You can download the example code files from your account at http://www.packtpub.com.

Our example is a simple alarm application that consists of two activities: MainActivity and SecondActivity. The MainActivity implements a self-built digital clock using text views and buttons. The purpose of creating a self-built digital clock is to have more code and elements to use in our tests. The layout of MainActivity is a relative one that includes two text views: one for the hour (the tvHour ID) and one for the minutes (the tvMinute ID). There are two buttons below the clock: one to subtract 10 minutes from the clock (the bMinus ID) and one to add 10 minutes to the clock (the bPlus ID). There is also an edit text field to specify the alarm name. Finally, there is a button to launch the second activity (the bValidate ID). Each button has a pertinent method that receives the click event when the button is pressed. The layout looks like the following screenshot:

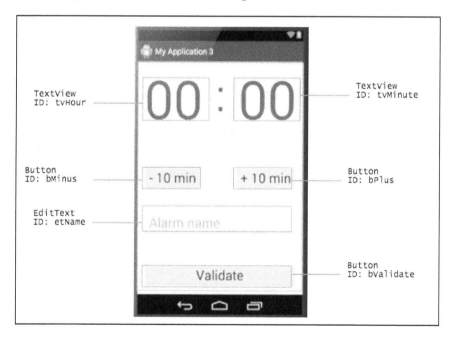

The SecondActivity receives the hour from the MainActivity and shows its value in a text view simulating that the alarm was saved. The objective to create this second activity is to be able to test the launch of another activity in our test case.

Open Android Studio and the Android project under test. You can create a blank project with a main activity and layout. Later in this chapter, we will add an example code to run the test cases. In the project structure, there is a folder and a package where the tests will be saved: `/src/androidTest/java/<your_package>`. If you don't have this package, you should add it.

Creating a unit test

A unit test evaluates the activity in isolation. Unit tests are used, for example, to check a method of the activity or to check that the activity has the correct layout. In this section, we are going to create a unit test for the main activity of our example project.

Create a new class in the test package of your application named `MainActivityUnitTest`. This class extends the `ActivityUnitTestCase` class, which is the test case class to create unit tests. The test class has to be parameterized with the activity under test and you also need to add the test case constructor, shown as follows:

```
public class MainActivityUnitTest
    extends ActivityUnitTestCase<MainActivity> {

    public MainActivityUnitTest() {
        super(MainActivity.class);
    }
}
```

For this unit test example, we will create the `setUp` method, and then we will test the buttons to manage the clock, main layout, and launch of the second activity.

The unit test setup

The fixture state of our test case includes the reference to the activity under test and the layout objects that will be used in the test methods, shown as follows:

```
private MainActivity mActivity;
private TextView mHour, mMinute;
private Button mValidate, mMinus, mPlus;
```

The `getActivity()` method initializes the activity under test, but remember that in unit tests, the activity is tested in isolation and therefore, it is not automatically started by the system. The activity has to be started in your own code via an `Intent` object. The code for the `setUp` method is as follows:

```
@Override
protected void setUp() throws Exception {
super.setUp();

Intent intent = new
    Intent(getInstrumentation().getTargetContext(),
    MainActivity.class);
startActivity(intent, null, null);
mActivity = getActivity();

mHour = (TextView) mActivity.findViewById(R.id.tvHour);
mMinute = (TextView) mActivity.findViewById(R.id.tvMinute);
mValidate = (Button) mActivity.findViewById(R.id.bValidate);
mMinus = (Button) mActivity.findViewById(R.id.bMinus);
mPlus = (Button) mActivity.findViewById(R.id.bPlus);
}
```

Layout elements are accessed by their ID as usual. Because the test code is included in a different package, you have to import the R class from the application package.

The clock test

Let's start implementing test methods. First, we will check whether the clock works properly. The test method consists of clicking on both the buttons, that is, **- 10 min** and **+ 10 min** and checking whether the values for the hour and minute texts are the expected ones. Since the activity runs in isolation, the TouchUtils library cannot be used, but the performClick method can be invoked instead, as follows:

```
public void testClock() {
  mMinus.performClick();
  assertEquals("11", mHour.getText());
  assertEquals("50", mMinute.getText());

  mPlus.performClick();
  mPlus.performClick();
  mMinus.performClick();
  assertEquals("00", mHour.getText());
  assertEquals("00", mMinute.getText());
}
```

From the default layout values, the initial hour is 00:00. On clicking the minus button once, the resultant hour is 11:50. On clicking the plus button twice and the minus button once, the final hour is again 00:00. The conditions are checked using the assertEquals method.

If you want to test complex UI events, do not use unit tests; you should create a functional test (ActivityInstrumentationTestCase2 test case).

The layout test

The second test method to be implemented is used to test whether the layout is correct. The text of the UI elements can be checked, or the assertion methods of the class ViewAsserts can also be invoked. A simple example of a UI test for our example is shown as follows:

```
public void testUI() {
    assertNotNull("Hour text view not found", mHour);
    assertEquals("Wrong button label", "Validate",
    mValidate.getText());
    ViewAsserts.assertBottomAligned(mHour, mMinute);
}
```

The activity Intent test

The last test method we will implement is going to check whether the second activity is properly launched. First, the **Validate** button is clicked to execute the code that will create Intent of the second activity. The getStartedActivityIntent method will return if any Intent was launched. The code snippet for the test method is as follows:

```
public void testSecondActivityLaunch() {
    mValidate.performClick();

    Intent triggeredIntent = getStartedActivityIntent();
    assertNotNull("Intent was null", triggeredIntent);

    String payload = triggeredIntent.getExtras().getString("hour");
    assertEquals("Wrong data passed to SecondActivity", "00",
    payload);
}
```

In the test method, Intent is checked to evaluate whether it is null. Furthermore, the data passed to the second activity can be examined as well.

The created Intent is not really sent to the system because the activity runs in isolation.

Creating a functional test

A functional test evaluates the activity and its communication with the Android system. The UI events or changes in the life cycle should be checked in a functional test. In this section, we will create a functional test for the main activity of our example project.

Create a new class in the test package of your application named `MainActivityTest`. This class extends the `ActivityInstrumentationTestCase2` class and has to be parameterized with the activity under test, shown as follows:

```
public class MainActivityTest
   extends ActivityInstrumentationTestCase2<MainActivity> {

   public MainActivityTest() {
     super(MainActivity.class);
   }
}
```

For this example of functional tests, we will evaluate the UI (white-box testing), launch of the second activity, and state management.

The functional test setup

The fixture state of our test case includes the reference to the activity under test and the layout objects that will be used in the test methods, shown as follows:

```
private MainActivity mActivity;
private TextView mHour, mMinute;
private Button mValidate;
private EditText mName;
```

Unlike unit testing, the `getActivity()` method is enough to start the activity under test. The `setUp` method code is shown as follows:

```
@Override
protected void setUp() throws Exception {
  super.setUp();

  setActivityInitialTouchMode(false);
  mActivity = getActivity();

  mHour = (TextView) mActivity.findViewById(R.id.tvHour);
  mMinute = (TextView) mActivity.findViewById(R.id.tvMinute);
  mValidate = (Button) mActivity.findViewById(R.id.bValidate);
  mName = (EditText) mActivity.findViewById(R.id.etName);
}
```

The setActivityInitialTouchMode method sets the initial touch mode for the activity. Setting the mode as false is necessary to set off the touch mode in the device so that the key events are not ignored. This method should be called before starting the activity with the getActivity method and also because it cannot be executed on the UI thread.

The UI test

In the first test method, as an example of UI testing, we will evaluate EditText containing the name of the alarm. The steps to be implemented for this test are as follows:

1. Request the focus of the edit text element. This step interacts with View of the application and therefore, it should run in the UI thread, that is, the main thread of the application. To run some code in the UI thread, you can use the runOnUiThread() method of the activity under test.

2. Send key events to write the alarm name. Only an instrumented class allows to send key events to the activity under test. Thanks to instrumentation, it is not necessary to run these calls in the UI thread either.

3. Test that the text of the edit field is the same as expected.

The UI test method is shown as follows:

```
public void testEditTextName() {
    mActivity.runOnUiThread(new Runnable() {
        public void run() {
            mName.requestFocus();
        }
    });

    sendKeys(KeyEvent.KEYCODE_A);
    sendKeys(KeyEvent.KEYCODE_L);
    sendKeys(KeyEvent.KEYCODE_1);

    getInstrumentation().waitForIdleSync();
    assertEquals("Wrong alarm name", "all",
    mName.getText().toString());
}
```

The waitForIdleSync method is called to wait for the application to be idle. Thus, we know for sure that the text has been completely inserted in the field.

The activity Intent test

Unlike unit tests, when a new Intent is created, it is sent to the Android system. To monitor the launched activity, we can register an `ActivityMonitor` object using instrumentation. Another difference between functional and unit tests is that in a functional test, we can use the `TouchUtils` library to send a click event on a UI element, shown as follows:

```
public void testSecondActivityLaunch() {
    Instrumentation.ActivityMonitor monitor =
    getInstrumentation().addMonitor(SecondActivity.class.getName(),
    null, false);

    TouchUtils.clickView(this, mValidate);

    SecondActivity secondActivity =
    (SecondActivity) monitor.waitForActivityWithTimeout(2000);
    assertNotNull(secondActivity);

    getInstrumentation().removeMonitor(monitor);
    sendKeys(KeyEvent.KEYCODE_BACK);
}
```

Our code performs the following steps for this test method:

1. Creates the activity monitor.
2. Sends a click event to the **Validate** button.
3. When the monitor receives the launched activity, it verifies that the activity was launched.
4. Deletes the monitor.
5. Closes the second activity by sending a click event to the device's back button.

The state management test

This last test method checks whether the activity state is preserved when the activity is, for example, paused or restarted. For this example, we will evaluate how our main activity behaves when it is paused and resumed. The expected behavior is that the hours and minutes are maintained. Performing a reliable test is necessary to directly change the text views between the pausing and resuming of the activity. This change ensures that the activity actually restores the previous state. The code of this method is as follows:

```
@UiThreadTest
public void testStateManagement() {
  mHour.setText("02");
  assertEquals("02", mHour.getText());

  getInstrumentation().callActivityOnPause(mActivity);
  mHour.setText("11");
  getInstrumentation().callActivityOnResume(mActivity);
  assertEquals("02", mHour.getText());
}
```

Notice the `@UiThreadTest` annotation before the method. Methods annotated with `@UiThreadTest` are executed in the UI thread. In the previous test method, the `setText` method on the text view has to be executed on the UI thread. If the `@UiThreadTest` annotation is not added, you have to use the `runOnUiThread()` method instead.

Getting the results

We already have an application and two test cases created in our Android project. The structure of the project can be seen in the following screenshot. Run the application once to check that there are no errors and install the application on the device. In this section, we will be running the test cases and examining the results.

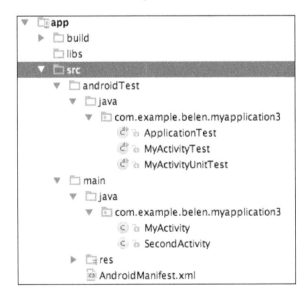

In Android Studio, select the package containing the test cases. Click on it using the right mouse button, and select the **Run 'Tests in <your_package>'** option. In the bottom part of Android Studio, open the **Run** tab to see the test execution. On the left part of this tab, you can inspect the test execution state. From the buttons on the left side, you can stop the test execution or rerun it. The next screenshot shows the initial state of the tests being initialized. On the right part of the tab, the commands and results are listed in the console.

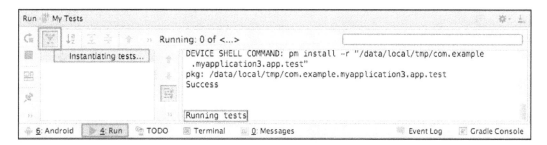

While a test method is being executed, it is also revealed on the left panel along with its execution state such as whether the test is still being evaluated, and whether the test was passed or not passed. When the test execution is completed, all the results are displayed. By deselecting the Hide Passed icon (highlighted in the previous screenshot), you can see all the test methods. Over the console, a color bar is also shown in green or red to indicate whether all the tests were passed or whether there were any fails. In our example, all the tests were passed as you can see in the following screenshot:

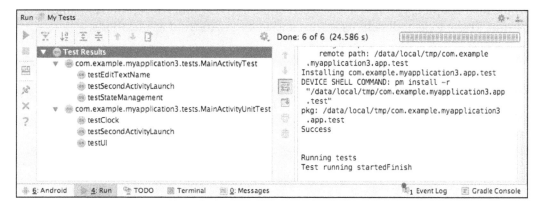

Try to insert an error in any test method, for example, by changing the following line of code from the `testStateManagement()` test method:

```
assertEquals("30", mMinute.getText());
```

Change the preceding line of code to the following:

```
assertEquals("40", mMinute.getText());
```

Run the tests and notice that now the fail is indicated in the results. The following screenshot shows how the fail is displayed:

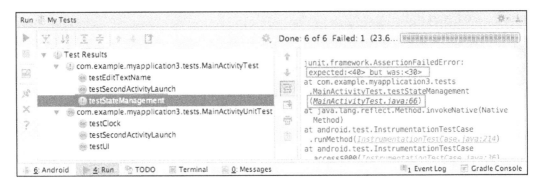

Summary

In this chapter, you learned more about Android testing. You now understand the structure of the Android testing API and we know its main classes and methods. You also learned about the importance of instrumentation to test activities of the Android applications. We set up the testing environment using Android Studio and followed the complete process of testing.

In the next chapter, you will learn about some external tools different from Android Studio. These tools will help us secure and test our Android applications.

10
Supporting Tools

In this chapter, you will learn about the external tools different from those available in Android Studio that will help us test our Android applications. The chapter will cover test tools to perform unit and functional tests. It will also cover tools that help us secure our application in different ways. We will end this chapter with an alternative tool that allows you to emulate an Android device.

The topics that are going to be covered in this chapter are:

- Tools for unit testing Android applications
- Tools for functional testing Android applications
- Tools for securing Android applications
- Some other tools

Tools for unit testing

As we have seen in *Chapter 9, Unit and Functional Tests*, unit testing is performed with minimal connection to the system infrastructure and tests the different components in isolation. We will see different tools that allow us to easily perform unit tests on Android applications. They are as follows:

- Spoon
- Mockito
- Android Mock
- FEST Android
- Robolectric

Spoon

Spoon is not a new form of unit testing. Instead, it makes use of the existing unit testing instrumentation such as JUnit to run tests on multiple devices. With Spoon, you can test your application on many devices at the same time. When the test is completed, you will receive a summary generated by Spoon with all the information regarding the test performed on the devices. You can also use Spoon for functional testing.

For a device to be considered by Spoon to run tests on, it has to be visible to the **Android Debug Bridge (adb)** devices. You can even perform the tests on different types of devices at the same time, such as smartphones, tablets, phablets, and so on, and in different versions of Android. The greater the diversity of the devices, the more useful the summary will be. With a big sample of devices, you can find more potential issues to be addressed. We can see an example with eight devices in the following figure:

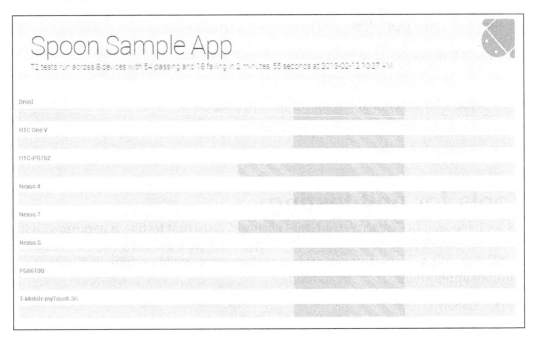

If you want to access the summary of the testing performed on a single device, you can do it with the **Device View**. Spoon makes a Device View available for each device in the sample so that you can see the results of a device individually. To access the Device View, you can simply click on the name of a device. We can see this view in the following figure:

If you want to access the summary of a specific test performed on all the devices in the sample, you can do it through the **Test View**. The Test View displays the result of a single test on every device. In case of an error, it will show the information that was generated by the error. To access the Test View, you can click on the icon with the shape of a smartphone on the Device View. We can see an example of this view in the following screenshot:

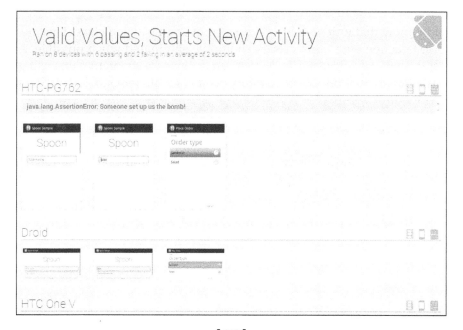

If you want to check the view of the application at any point in time, you can use the **Screenshot** feature. This feature allows you to take a screenshot of the information being displayed to the user at any given moment during the execution. The screenshots are available in both the Device View if you want to see all the screenshots taken in a single device, and the Test View if you want to see the screenshots taken of each test in every device.

To make use of this feature, you need to include the `spoon-client.jar` library in your application. When you want to take a screenshot, you can call the static `screenshot(Activity, String)` method of the `Spoon` class, shown as follows:

```
Spoon.screenshot(activity, "login_activity");
```

> If you want to know more about Spoon or want to download the tool, you can follow this link:
>
> `http://square.github.io/spoon/`

Mockito

Mockito is a mock testing framework for Java that can be used in conjunction with JUnit and other unit testing frameworks. It has been compatible with Android since Version 1.9.5. Mockito allows the use of automatic unit testing to enhance the quality of our code. Most unit testing frameworks are based on an **expect-run-verify** pattern. Mockito removes the specification of expectations reducing the pattern to run-verify.

We already know that unit tests are performed over an isolated class. This means that their interaction with other classes should be eliminated when possible. As seen in *Chapter 9, Unit and Functional Tests,* you can achieve these interactions using mock objects also known as stubs. Mockito allows you to create mock objects using the `mock()` method.

You can also initialize a mock object using the `@Mock` annotation and the `MockitoAnnotations` class. You can call the `MockitoAnnotations.initMocks()` method to initiate the mock objects that were defined with the `@Mock` annotation.

The `verify()` method can be called on a `mock` object to verify that a certain method was called. To specify a condition and a return value when the condition is met, you can use the `when()` method in conjunction with the `thenReturn()` method.

For example, let's say we want to check whether the `test` method was called in the following code:

```
// Create the mock object
TestClass testClassMock = Mockito.mock(TestClass.class);

// Call a method on the mock object
boolean result = testClassMock.test("hello world");

// Test the return value
assertTrue (result);

// Check that the method test() was called
Mockito.verify(testClassMock).test("hello world");
```

Mockito cannot be used to test final classes, anonymous classes, and primitive types.

> If you want to learn more about Mockito, visit its website: `https://code.google.com/p/mockito/`

Android Mock

Android Mock is similar to Mockito. Android Mock is also a framework to mock classes and interfaces. It works with the Android Dalvik Virtual Machine. It is based on the Java mocking framework EasyMock and uses the same grammar and syntax.

In order to learn about the grammar and syntax of Android Mock, we will repeat the same example as we did with Mockito:

```
public class MockingTest extends TestCase {
  // Create the mock object
  @UsesMocks(TestClass.class)
  TestClass testClassMock =
  AndroidMock.createMock(TestClass.class);

  // Tells the mock object that the method test will be called and
  // the value true will be expected
  AndroidMock.expect(testClassMock.test("hello
  world")).andReturn(true);
```

```
    // Make the mock object ready to be tested
    AndroidMock.replay(testClassMock);

    // Test the return value
    assertTrue (testClassMock.test("hello world"));

    // Test that the method test() was called
    AndroidMock.verify(testClassMock);
}
```

As you can see, the main difference in Android Mock and Mockito is that Android
Mock follows the pattern expectation-run-verify.

 If you want to learn more about Android Mock, you can visit the
project website: `https://code.google.com/p/android-mock/`.

FEST Android

FEST Android is a library that extends the FEST functionality to Android. FEST is a
unit test framework for Java. It is basically a simpler form of making assertions. In the
following code, we see the differences between JUnit, FEST, and FEST for Android:

```
    // Assertion using JUNIT
    assertEquals(View.GONE, view.getVisibility());

    // Assertion using FEST
    assertThat(view.getVisibility()).isEqualTo(View.GONE);

    // Assertion using FEST for Android
    assertThat(view).isGone();
```

FEST for Android offers assertions that are executed directly on objects instead
of properties. This makes it possible to chain together several assertions, shown
as follows:

```
    assertThat(layout).isVisible().isVertical().hasChildCount(3);
```

There are many available assertions for typical Android objects, such as
`LinearLayout`, `ActionBar`, `Fragment`, and `MenuItem`.

 If you want to learn more about FEST, you can visit the project website
at `https://code.google.com/p/fest/`. If you want to learn more
about FEST for Android, you can visit the URL at `http://square.`
`github.io/fest-android/`.

Robolectric

Robolectric allows you to run unit tests of your Android application on your workstation's Java Virtual Machine. This has one main advantage, that is, speed. Running unit tests in Android means that the application needs to be loaded either on the Android emulator or on your device.

Robolectric takes a different path than mock frameworks such as Mockito and instead of mocking out the Android SDK, Robolectric rewrites the Android SDK classes and makes it possible to run them on a regular JVM. It can, however, be used in conjunction with mocking testing frameworks such as Mockito or Android Mock.

Robolectric makes use of the @RunWith annotation from JUnit 4, shown as follows:

```
@RunWith(RobolectricTestRunner.class)
public class Test1 {
  // Your tests
}
```

 If you want to learn more about Robolectric, you can visit the project website at http://robolectric.org/.

Tools for functional testing

In *Chapter 9*, *Unit and Functional Tests*, you learned how functional tests are performed with full connection to the system infrastructure. In this section, we will look at the different tools that allow us to easily perform functional tests in Android applications:

- Robotium
- Espresso
- Appium
- Calabash
- MonkeyTalk
- Bot-bot
- Monkey
- Wireshark

Robotium

Robotium runs on the official Android testing framework. It adds the necessary features to run through an entire Android application. It has full support for both native and hybrid applications.

Now, we will see the steps needed to run a test using Robotium on our Android application:

1. Add the `Robotium` JAR to your Build Path.
2. Create a test case using the JUnit `TestCase` class.
3. Write the test case code.
4. Run the test case.

Tests with Robotium are performed using the `com.robotium.solo.Solo` class available in the `Robotium` library.

We will now see an example of the white-box testing using Robotium. In this example, we have two `EditText` fields: one where the user can input a numeric value `ValueEditText` and another one that will display the value of the input multiplied by 2, `ResultEditText`. The multiplication is made when the **Button1** button is clicked:

```
public class TestMain extends
    ActivityInstrumentationTestCase2<MainActivity> {

  // Declaration of the Solo object
  private Solo mSolo;

  // Constructor
  public TestMain() {
    super(Main.class);
  }

  // Set Up
  @Override
  protected void setUp() throws Exception {
    super.setUp();
    // Initiate the instance of Solo
    mSolo = new Solo(getInstrumentation(), getActivity());
  }
```

```
// White-Box Test Code
public void testWhiteBox() {
  EditText valueEditText =
    (EditText) solo.getView(R.id.ValueEditText);
  EditText resultEditText =
    (EditText) solo.getView(R.id.ResultEditText);

  // Clears the Edit Text
  mSolo.clearEditText(valueEditText);
  // Sets the value of the EditText to 10
  mSolo.enterText(valueEditText, String.valueOf(10));

  // Clicks on Button1
  mSolo.clickOnButton("Button1");

  // Assert to check if it worked
  assertEquals(String.valueOf(20),
    resultEditText.getText().toString());
  }
}
```

 If you want to learn more about Robotium, you can visit the project website at https://code.google.com/p/robotium/. If you want to learn how to use Robotium, we recommend the official getting started guide: https://code.google.com/p/robotium/wiki/Getting_Started.

Espresso

Espresso is an API that lets you test state expectations, assertions, and interactions. There are many actions that can be performed with Espresso using a simple syntax. Let's see how the example we used for Robotium will be executed with Espresso:

```
public void testWhiteBox() {

  // Type the text "10" in the ValueEditText
  onView(withId(R.id.ValueEditText)).perform(typeText("10"));

  // Click the button Button1
  onView(withId(R.id.Button1)).perform(click());

  // Check if the value displayed is "20"
  onView(withText("20").check(matches(isDisplayed())));
}
```

To make use of the `Espresso` library in Android Studio, you need to follow these steps:

1. Add the `Espresso` JAR as a library dependency.

2. Add this instrumentation to your project `AndroidManifest.xml`:

   ```
   <instrumentation
   android:name="com.google.android.apps.common.testing.testrunner.
   GoogleInstrumentationTestRunner"
   android:targetPackage="YOUR_PACKAGE"/>
   ```

3. Configure tests to run with `GoogleInstrumentationTestRunner`.

 If you want to learn more about Espresso, you can visit the project website at `https://code.google.com/p/android-test-kit/wiki/Espresso`. If you have 15 minutes to spare, we recommend their Google Test Automation Conference 2013 presentation at `https://www.youtube.com/watch?v=T7ugmCuNxDU`.

Appium

Appium is an open source framework that allows automated testing. Appium works with both native and hybrid Android applications. It even works with iOS. Appium is a good solution if you need to test in both Android and iOS.

 To download or just learn more about Appium, you can visit their website at `http://appium.io/`. If you want to see examples for Appium, visit their GitHub at `https://github.com/appium/appium/tree/master/sample-code/examples`.

Calabash

Just like Appium, Calabash is also a multiplatform framework that performs automated tests. It works with Android native applications, hybrid applications, and iOS native applications. Calabash allows you to take screenshots of the current view in a determined instant. One of the things that separate Calabash from the other testing frameworks is that it supports **Cucumber**. Cucumber allows people with less expertise in this matter to easily define the behavior of the application using natural language, for example:

```
When I touch the "addition" button
Then I should see "20"
```

The Calabash tool is based on `ActivityInstrumentationTestCase2` from the Android SDK.

 If you want to know more about Calabash, you can visit the project website: `http://calaba.sh/`. To learn more about the Cucumber project, visit their website: `http://cukes.info/`.

MonkeyTalk

MonkeyTalk is yet another multiplatform automated test framework. MonkeyTalk supports more features than Appium and Calabash. However, the version with every feature available is a subscription-licensed product that is currently offered in a free beta version but will be charged when the beta is over.

 If you want to download MonkeyTalk or just learn more about it, you can visit the project website at `http://www.cloudmonkeymobile.com/monkeytalk`. To see an example using the MonkeyTalk framework with an Android application, watch the following YouTube video: `https://www.youtube.com/watch?v=pjDGctTnThQ`.

Bot-bot

Bot-bot is an Android automation testing tool with two interesting features: record and replay. You do not need to add any kind of library or dependency to your project, since the only thing bot-bot needs is an APK of the application you want to test. The record feature allows you to store the sequence of events that were triggered. It works both on a simulator and a real device. The recorded test cases can be exported in the CSV format and replayed using the bot-bot tool.

Bot-bot consists of three elements:

- **The bot-bot server**: This server is used to store and modify the actions taken on the Android application. It includes a simple HTML interface that allows you to view recorded sessions, view recorded entries of a session, modify or create assertions, export recorded sessions in CSV, and delete recorded sessions.

- **The bot-bot recorder**: This recorder tracks the user actions on the Android application that are being tested, and sends these tasks to the bot-bot server. It supports recording of actions on TextBoxes, Adapters, and Spinners. It also records clicks on elements and views. It does not support actions on WebViews.

- **The bot-bot runner**: This runner takes the exported sessions in the CSV format and interprets them. The bot-bot runner then executes the actions on the Android application and generates an HTML report that shows the execution of the test cases defined.

The following screenshot shows an example of a generated HTML report by the bot-bot runner:

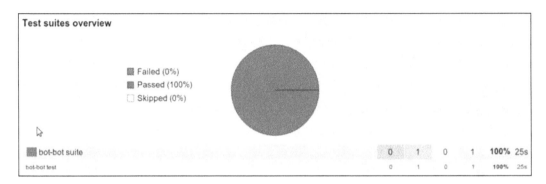

Bot-bot is perfectly integrated with Robotium.

> If you want to download the bot-bot application, you can visit their website: http://imaginea.github.io/bot-bot/. To learn how to use the bot-bot tool, we recommend the official *Get Started* guide: http://imaginea.github.io/bot-bot/pages/get_started.html.

Monkey

Monkey is a command-line tool that runs on your Android emulator or device. It generates random user events and system-level events to stress test your application. Although the interactions are random, they are based on a seeding system and therefore you can repeat the same sequence of actions using the same seed. This is important since otherwise, you would not be able to repeat the sequence that produced an error to check whether it was fixed.

There are four main categories of options in Monkey:

- **Basic configuration options**: An example of this can be the help or verbosity level

- **Operational constraints**: An example of this can be the packages in which the stress test will be performed

- **Event types**: An example of this can be the number of events, random seed, and delay between events

- **Debugging options**: An example of this can be killing the process after an error or ignoring the security exceptions

To launch the Monkey, you need to use a command line on your development machine shown as follows:

```
adb shell monkey -p com.packt.package -v 100
```

The -p argument states the package where the Monkey will send random events. The -v parameter states the number of random events that will be sent.

> There are many other parameters for Monkey. If you want to learn about these parameters, you can visit the official Android guide: http://developer.android.com/tools/help/monkey. html.

Wireshark

Wireshark, formerly known as Ethereal, is a protocol analyzer used to perform analysis and solve problems related to network connectivity. Its functionality is similar to the tool **tcpdump**, but Wireshark provides a more intuitive GUI.

You can use Wireshark in combination with your Android emulator to check what information is being transferred to and from your Android application. The main issue with this tool is that you need to know what packages to expect, since otherwise the task of filtering can become really difficult. The best advice we can give is to close the browser and other programs in your computer that may generate network traffic to keep it to a minimum.

In this book, we already discussed Wireshark in *Chapter 6, Securing Communications*. One of the topics we discussed was that we can use Wireshark to test whether the data we are sending is being encrypted properly or not. Other alternatives to Wireshark are Fiddler for Windows and Charles proxy for OS X. A screenshot of Wireshark is shown in the following figure:

Time	Source	Destination	Protocol	Length	Info
.015662000	192.168.1.7	91.198.174.202	TCP	78	51983 > https [SYN] Seq=0 Win=65535 Len=0 MSS=1460 WS=16 TSval=600
.015752000	192.168.1.7	91.198.174.202	TCP	78	51984 > https [SYN] Seq=0 Win=65535 Len=0 MSS=1460 WS=16 TSval=600
.015841000	192.168.1.7	91.198.174.202	TCP	78	51985 > https [SYN] Seq=0 Win=65535 Len=0 MSS=1460 WS=16 TSval=600
.016121000	192.168.1.7	91.198.174.208	TCP	78	51986 > https [SYN] Seq=0 Win=65535 Len=0 MSS=1460 WS=16 TSval=600
.016207000	192.168.1.7	91.198.174.208	TCP	78	51987 > https [SYN] Seq=0 Win=65535 Len=0 MSS=1460 WS=16 TSval=600
.016273000	192.168.1.7	91.198.174.208	TCP	78	51988 > https [SYN] Seq=0 Win=65535 Len=0 MSS=1460 WS=16 TSval=600
.016334000	192.168.1.7	91.198.174.208	TCP	78	51989 > https [SYN] Seq=0 Win=65535 Len=0 MSS=1460 WS=16 TSval=600
.016396000	192.168.1.7	91.198.174.208	TCP	78	51990 > https [SYN] Seq=0 Win=65535 Len=0 MSS=1460 WS=16 TSval=600
.077811000	91.198.174.192	192.168.1.7	TCP	74	https > 51981 [SYN, ACK] Seq=0 Ack=1 Win=14480 Len=0 MSS=1452 SACK
.077912000	192.168.1.7	91.198.174.192	TCP	66	51981 > https [ACK] Seq=1 Ack=1 Win=132480 Len=0 TSval=600190552
.078144000	192.168.1.7	91.198.174.192	TLSv1.2	583	Client Hello
.082017000	91.198.174.202	192.168.1.7	TCP	74	https > 51982 [SYN, ACK] Seq=0 Ack=1 Win=14480 Len=0 MSS=1452 SACK
.082089000	192.168.1.7	91.198.174.202	TCP	66	51982 > https [ACK] Seq=1 Ack=1 Win=132480 Len=0 TSval=600190556

```
▷ Frame 231: 78 bytes on wire (624 bits), 78 bytes captured (624 bits) on interface 0
▽ Ethernet II, Src: Apple_1a:f2:1a (b8:e8:56:1a:f2:1a), Dst: CameoCom_27:03:7c (18:17:25:27:03:7c)

0000  18 17 25 27 03 7c b8 e8  56 1a f2 1a 08 00 45 00   ..%'.|.. V.....E.
0010  00 40 32 d6 40 00 40 06  3b 9c c0 a8 01 07 5b c6   .@2.@.@. ;.....[.
0020  ae d0 cb 17 01 bb bc 0d  c8 e4 00 00 00 00 b0 02   ........ ........
0030  ff ff c7 11 00 00 02 04  05 b4 01 03 03 04 01 01   ........ ........
0040  08 0a 23 c6 2e 1b 00 00  00 00 04 02 00 00         ..#..... ......
```

 If you want to download or learn more about Wireshark, visit their website: http://www.wireshark.org/.

Other tools

In this last section, we will see a tool that is not directly related to application testing or security testing. However, it can significantly improve our testing experience.

Genymotion

Genymotion is an alternative and unofficial Android emulator. It is basically a virtual emulator that creates a virtual image of Android and is often considered much faster than the official Android emulator. It is available for Windows, Linux, and Mac OS. If you are using Windows or Linux, you only need to install the Genymotion distribution package. However, if you are using Mac OS, you need to download and install VirtualBox manually. The following is a screenshot captured from the virtual device manager that lists all the virtual devices available:

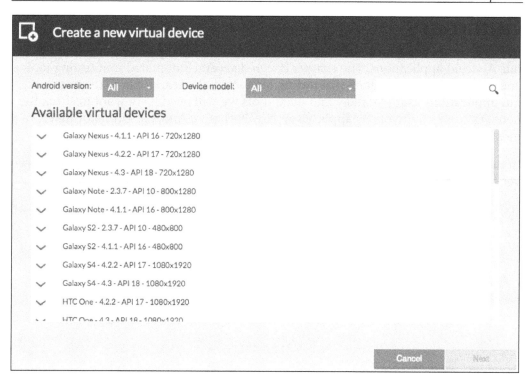

If you want to get started with using Genymotion, you can visit our blog: `http://belencruz.com/2014/01/first-look-at-genymotion-android-emulator/`. To download and learn more about Genymotion, visit the project website: `http://www.genymotion.com/`. If you are using Mac OS and need to download VirtualBox, follow this link: `https://www.virtualbox.org/`.

Summary

In this chapter, you learned about the external tools that help us perform tests on our Android applications. The chapter covered several automated unit testing tools and several automated functional testing tools. You also learned how to stress test our applications using Monkey and what tools we will need if we want to check the network connectivity of our application. An alternative Android emulator that is in most cases faster than the official one was reviewed too.

In the next chapter, which is the last chapter, you will learn about some tips that are very useful for developers. You will also learn how to get help in case you need it.

11
Further Considerations

This chapter provides some further considerations that are useful for developers. We will review what are the most important parts of our application that we need to test. This chapter also contains information about how to get help for more advanced topics.

The topics that will be covered in this chapter are:

- What to test
- Developer options
- Getting help

What to test

In the previous chapters, you learned about the Android testing API working with Android Studio. Apart from knowing about activity and UI testing, considering what parts of your application should be evaluated is also important.

Network access

If your application depends on the network access, you should examine the behavior of your application when different network states are given. Consider the following suggestions:

- If your application completely depends on the network when it is launched and there is no network access, it should at least show a default home screen. Your application should not show a blank screen with any information on it. Let the user know that he/she should review the device connectivity. The network state can be checked using the `ConnectivityManager` class in the following code:

```
ConnectivityManager connManager = (ConnectivityManager)
  getSystemService(Context.CONNECTIVITY_SERVICE);
NetworkInfo netInfo = connManager.getActiveNetworkInfo();
if (netInfo != null && netInfo.isConnected()) {
  // Connect
} else {
  // display default screen
}
```

- When there are problems accessing the network that affect the normal behavior of your application, let the user know this by displaying a message.

- When performing long network operations, the user should also be able to use your application. Check that your application continues working properly even while performing long network operations.

- Your application's data should maintain its consistency. If your application sends or receives any kind of information to or from your server, this information should be correctly synchronized. Check that your application and server can recover from a network failure and maintain the consistency of your application's data.

- To mitigate network failures, your application can cache some of the information. Check the management of the cached information and its usage when there is no network access.

- A good policy is to change the behavior of your application depending on the type of network access, for example, it should be able to detect whether the device is connected to a Wi-Fi or 3G network and work accordingly. You should test whether your application follows the defined policy and whether it is able to react to changes in the connection type. The connection type can be checked using the following code:

```
boolean wifiConnected =
  netInfo.getType() == ConnectivityManager.TYPE_WIFI;
boolean mobileConnected =
  netInfo.getType() == ConnectivityManager.TYPE_MOBILE;
```

- If there is a network failure, your application should retry after a while. You should check which behavior is appropriate for your application and whether it is capable of recovering from failures.

Media availability

If your application depends on external media, your code should check the availability of that media. While designing your tests, you should evaluate whether your application behaves correctly if the media is not available.

For example, if your application works with an external storage, you can check its state by using the `Environment.getExternalStorageState` method, as it was shown in *Chapter 5*, *Preserving Data Privacy*. To test the external storage availability, you can configure the AVD to run on the emulator from Android Studio, as it is shown in the following screenshot:

Change in orientation

If a device supports multiple orientations, your application should be prepared for the same. You have to decide whether your application will block the orientation changes or not. If your application supports orientation changes, consider the following suggestions:

- When there is an orientation change, the current activity is destroyed and restarted. Check that the activity state is maintained. For example, if your activity contains an input field that the user can edit, its content has to be preserved when the device orientation changes.

- Your UI should also adapt to the device's current orientation. The position and distribution of your UI elements are different on a portrait orientation than on a landscape one. You should check that the design of your UI is perfectly displayed in both the orientations.

You can change the emulator orientation by pressing *Ctrl* + *F11* in Windows or Linux, or *Fn* + *Ctrl* + *F11* in Mac OS. To check the orientation changes, you can override the onConfigurationChanged method of your activities, shown as follows:

```
@Override
public void onConfigurationChanged(Configuration newConfig) {
  super.onConfigurationChanged(newConfig);

  if (newConfig.orientation ==
    Configuration.ORIENTATION_LANDSCAPE) {
  ...
} else if (newConfig.orientation ==
  Configuration.ORIENTATION_PORTRAIT){
  ...
  }
}
```

Service and content provider testing

In Android, we can test the UI, activities, services, and content providers. In *Chapter 9, Unit and Functional Tests*, activity testing was explained. But you should not forget about services testing and content providers testing. The classes in the Android testing API used to evaluate services and content providers are listed in the following figure:

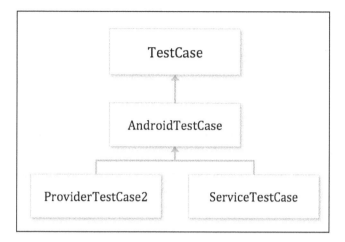

The `AndroidTestCase` class and its subclasses belong to the `android.test` package. It represents a test case to be used in the Android environment. Since this class is generic, you should use one of its subclasses. The `ProviderTestCase2` class is used to test content providers. The `ServiceTestCase` class is used to test services.

Developer options

The Android system provides a set of on-device developer options that will help you test your application. These options are available in the **Settings** menu of any Android device. On Android 4.2 and higher, the developer options are hidden. Click on the **About phone** option in the **Settings** menu and click on the **Build number** seven times to make them available. The following screenshot shows the **Developer options** in Android's **Settings** menu:

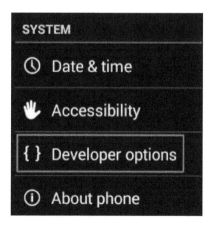

The **Developer options** are organized into seven categories, described as follows:

- **General**: This option is not present in any category. For example, you can get a bug report by selecting the **Take bug report** option.

- **Debugging**: This category includes useful tools to debug your application. For example, when you want to test your application on a real device, you should check the USB debugging option contained in this category. You can also select a debug app (**Select debug app**) or allow mock locations (**Allow mock locations**).

- **Input**: This category contains two tools. These are **Show touches** to provide a visual feedback for touches on the screen, and **Pointer location** to overlay the touch data on the screen.

- **Drawing**: This category includes options to change the graphical behavior of the application and the system itself, such as **Show surface updates**, **Show layout bounds, Force RTL layout direction**, and **Simulate secondary displays**. You may want to disable animations that take place when an application is opened. To do so, you can set to **Animation off** the following options: **Window animation scale, Transition animation scale**, and **Animator duration scale**.

- **Hardware accelerated rendering**: In this section, you can change the behavior of the **Graphics Processing Unit (GPU)**. The options available are **Force GPU rendering, Show GPU view updates, Show hardware layers updates, Debug GPU overdraw, Debug non-rectangular clip operation, Force 4xMSAA**, and **Disable HW overlays**.

- **Monitoring**: This category contains options that allow you to track possible problems or malfunctions. The options available are **Strict mode enabled, Show CPU usage, Profile GPU rendering**, and **Enable OpenGL traces**.

- **Apps**: This category includes options to manage the behavior of applications when they are running in the background. Activating **Don't keep activities** will destroy every activity when the user leaves it. The background process limit allows you to control the number of processes that can be executed in the background. If you activate the option **Show all ANRs**, applications will display a dialog when they don't respond.

Getting help

If you want to access the Android Studio documentation, you can do it through the IntelliJ IDEA web help. You can go to **Help | Online Documentation**, or access the web page http://www.jetbrains.com/idea/documentation/. You can also go to **Help | Help Topics** to directly open the documentation contents tree, or visit the web page http://www.jetbrains.com/idea/webhelp/intellij-idea.html.

Android's official documentation is provided by Google and is available at http://developer.android.com/. The Android documentation includes every kind of guide to learn how to program Android applications. It also includes design guidelines and even tips on distributing and promoting your application.

Some of the important references of all the previous chapters are listed as follows:

- *Chapter 1, Introduction to Software Security*:
    - *Glossary of terms* at http://www.sans.org/security-resources/glossary-of-terms/

- *Chapter 2, Security in Android Applications*:
    - *Content providers* at http://developer.android.com/guide/topics/providers/content-providers.html
    - *Intent filters* at http://developer.android.com/guide/components/intents-filters.html

- *Chapter 3, Monitoring Your Application*:
    - *DDMS* at http://developer.android.com/tools/debugging/ddms.html

- *Chapter 4, Mitigating Vulnerabilities*:
    - *The Pattern class* at http://developer.android.com/reference/java/util/regex/Pattern.html
    - *Storing data* at http://developer.android.com/training/articles/security-tips.html#StoringData

- *Chapter 5, Preserving Data Privacy*:
  - ○ *Cipher* at `http://developer.android.com/reference/javax/crypto/Cipher.html`
  - ○ *Storage options* at `http://developer.android.com/guide/topics/data/data-storage.html#filesInternal`

- *Chapter 6, Securing Communications*:
  - ○ *Using cryptography* at `http://developer.android.com/training/articles/security-tips.html#Crypto`
  - ○ *Security with HTTPS and SSL* at `http://developer.android.com/training/articles/security-ssl.html`

- *Chapter 7, Authentication Methods*:
  - ○ *AccountManager* at `http://developer.android.com/reference/android/accounts/AccountManager.html`

- *Chapter 8, Testing Your Application*:
  - ○ *UI testing* at `http://developer.android.com/tools/testing/testing_ui.html`
  - ○ *uiautomator* at `http://developer.android.com/tools/help/uiautomator/index.html`

- *Chapter 9, Unit and Functional Tests*:
  - ○ *Creating unit tests* at `http://developer.android.com/training/activity-testing/activity-unit-testing.html`
  - ○ *Creating functional tests* at `http://developer.android.com/training/activity-testing/activity-functional-testing.html`
  - ○ *ViewAsserts* at `http://developer.android.com/reference/android/test/ViewAsserts.html`
  - ○ *MoreAsserts* at `http://developer.android.com/reference/android/test/MoreAsserts.html`

- *Chapter 10, Supporting Tools*:

  - ° *Spoon* at http://square.github.io/spoon/
  - ° *Mockito* at https://code.google.com/p/mockito/
  - ° *Android Mock* at https://code.google.com/p/android-mock/
  - ° *FEST Android* at http://square.github.io/fest-android/
  - ° *Robolectric* at http://robolectric.org/
  - ° *Robotium* at https://code.google.com/p/robotium/
  - ° *Espresso* at https://code.google.com/p/android-test-kit/wiki/Espresso
  - ° *Appium* at http://appium.io/
  - ° *Calabash* at http://calaba.sh/
  - ° *MonkeyTalk* at http://www.cloudmonkeymobile.com/monkeytalk
  - ° *Bot-bot* at http://imaginea.github.io/bot-bot/
  - ° *Monkey* at http://developer.android.com/tools/help/monkey.html
  - ° *Wireshark* at http://www.wireshark.org/
  - ° *Genymotion* at http://www.genymotion.com/

Summary

In this chapter, you learned about which parts of our application are more important to evaluate and test. We reviewed the developer options available in Android and how to access them. We also learned how to get additional help using the official documentation and other sources.

Index

asymmetric encryption 56
authentication 6
authentication factors
  inherence factor 77
  knowledge factor 76
  possession factor 77
authorization 6
availability 6

B

basis path testing 13
biometric authentication 77
biometric identifiers
  behavioral characteristics 77
  physiological characteristics 77
black-box tests
  about 12, 84
  all pairs testing 14
  boundary value analysis 13
  cause-effect graphing 14
  equivalence partitioning 13
  state transition testing 14
  syntax testing 14
bot-bot
  about 121, 122
  bot-bot recorder 121
  bot-bot runner 122
  bot-bot server 121
  URL, for downloading 122
boundary value analysis technique 13
broadcast messages, types
  normal 23
  ordered 23
  sticky 23
broadcast receivers 22
brute force 6

C

Calabash 120
categories, developer options
  Apps 132
  Debugging 132
  Drawing 132
  General 132

Hardware accelerated rendering 132
  Input 132
  Monitoring 132
cause-effect graphing technique 14
certificate
  about 20, 67
  creating 67
  using 67
Certificate Authority (CA) 71
Cipher 6
code injection 6
confidentiality 6
Console 28
content providers
  about 25
  securing 48
  securing, precautions 48
  testing 130, 131
  URL, for official documentation 25
control flow testing 13
crack 6
cross-site scripting (XSS) 10
cryptographic keys 77

D

Dalvik Debug Monitor Server. *See* DDMS
dangerous permission level 45
data
  storing, encryption used 59, 60
database storage 55
Data Encryption Standard (DES) 66
data flow testing 13
data privacy 51, 52
DDMS 28
debugger 28
debugging 28
decryption 6
Denial-of-service (DoS) 7
developer options
  about 131
  categories 132
Device View 112
dictionary attack 7
Distributed denial-of-service (DDoS) 7
doFinal method 57

E

electronic commerce (e-commerce) 6
Emulator Control tab
  about 40
  Location Controls 40
  Telephony Actions 40
  Telephony Status 40
encryption
  about 7, 56, 57
  asymmetric encryption 56
  key, generating 58, 59
  symmetric encryption 56
  used, for storing data 59, 60
  using 57, 58
equivalence partitioning technique 13
Espresso
  about 119
  reference link 120
exclusive time 31
expect-run-verify pattern 114
external storage
  about 55
  private files 55
  public files 55

F

fabrication, threat 8
features, Android security
  application-defined permissions 20
  application signing 20
  encrypted file system 20
  interprocess communication 20
  support for cryptography 20
  support for secure networking 20
FEST Android
  about 116
  URL 116
File Explorer tab 39
File Transfer Protocol (FTP) 64
functional tests. *See also* **black-box tests**
  about 93
  activity Intent test method,
    implementing 107
  creating 105
  setting up 105

state management test method,
  implementing 107
tools, using 117
UI test method, implementing 106

G

garbage collector (GC) 33
Genymotion
  about 124
  URL 125
getAccountsByName method 81
getActivity() method 95, 102
getContentResolver().query() method
  about 25
  content URI 25
  projection 25
  selection 25
  selection arguments 25
  sort order 25
getInstrumentation() method 95
getPreferences() method 52
getSharedPreferences() method 52
getTargetContext method 96
getUiDevice() method 85
Graphics Processing Unit (GPU) 132

H

hash function 7
Heap tab
  displaying 33, 34
help, Android Studio
  obtaining 133
Hijack attack 7
HTTP
  versus HTTPS 65
Hypertext Transfer Protocol Secure
    (HTTPS)
  about 7, 63-65
  Android Studio 70
  certificate, creating 67
  examples 71, 72
  Keytool 68, 69
  SSL 66
  TLS 66
  versus HTTP 65

mode flag, internal storage
  MODE_APPEND 54
  MODE_PRIVATE 54
  MODE_WORLD_READABLE 54
  MODE_WORLD_WRITEABLE 54
modification, threat 8
Monkey
  about 122, 123
  basic configuration options 123
  debugging options 123
  event types 123
  operational constraints 123
  URL, for parameters 123
MonkeyTalk
  about 121
  URL, for downloading 121
MoreAsserts class
  about 98, 99
  assertContainsRegex() method 98
  assertContentsInAnyOrder() method 99
  assertContentsInOrder() method 99
  assertEmpty() method 99
  assertEquals() method 99
  assertMatchesRegex() method 99
  URL 99
multifactor authentication 75
my_keystore.jks file 69
MyPrefsFile file 53
MyReadablePrefsFile file 53
MyWriteablePrefsFile file 53

N

network access
  testing 127, 128
Network Statistics tab
  displaying 36-38
normal broadcast 23
normal permission level 45

O

onCreate method 96
openFileOutput() method 54
open source software (OSS) 66
Open Systems Interconnection model. See
    OSI model

operating mode, shared preferences
  MODE_PRIVATE 52
  MODE_WORLD_READABLE 52
operating system (OS) 17
ordered broadcast 23
orientation changes
  testing 130
OSI model
  about 64
  versus TCP/IP model 64

P

password 7
pattern 76
Pattern class
  DOMAIN_NAME pattern 42
  EMAIL_ADDRESS pattern 42
  IP_ADDRESS pattern 42
  PHONE pattern 42
  TOP_LEVEL_DOMAIN pattern 42
  WEB_URL pattern 42
PBKDF2 algorithm 60
permission level
  dangerous 45
  normal 45
  signature 45
  signatureOrSystem 45
permissions 20, 44, 45
phishing 7
physical layer 64
PIN 76
possession factor 77
private files 55
public files 55

R

regular expressions
  URL, for documentation 42
resourceId method 90
risk 7, 10
Robolectric
  about 117
  URL 117
Robotium
  about 118, 119
  reference link 119

S

Screenshot feature 114
SecretKeySpec class 58
secure code-design, principles
  address vulnerabilities 12
  clarity 11
  failing securely 12
  least privileges 11
  secure defaults 11
  simplicity 12
  small surface area 11
  strong defense 11
  no trust, on third-party companies 12
SecureRandom class 58
Secure Sockets Layer. *See* SSL
security testing
  about 12
  black-box tests 12
  white-box tests 12
sensitive data 51
service
  about 22
  testing 130, 131
setUp() method 96
SHA1 7
shared preferences 52-54
signatureOrSystem permission level 45
signature permission level 45
Simple Mail Transfer Protocol. *See* SMTP
smartphone
  about 18
  vulnerabilities 18
SMTP 64
sniffing attack 7
software security
  terms 6-8
specification testing. *See* black-box tests
spoofing attack 7
Spoon
  about 112-114
  URL, for downloading 114
spoon-client.jar library 114
SQL 25
SQL injection 10, 43, 44
SSL 65, 66
SSL 3.0 66

SSL connection
  establishing 66
SSLHandshakeException 73
startActivitySync method 96
statement coverage 13
State transition testing technique 14
sticky broadcast 23
storage options
  database storage 52, 55
  external storage 52, 55
  internal storage 52, 54
  shared preferences 52-54
Structural Query Language. *See* SQL
structural tests. *See* white-box tests
symmetric cryptography 7
symmetric encryption 56
Syntax testing technique 14
System Information tab 40
system tests 14

T

tcpdump 123
TCP/IP model
  about 64
  application layer 64
  internet layer 64
  link layer 64
  physical layer 64
  transport layer 64
  versus OSI model 64
tearDown() method 96
terms, software security
  access control 6
  asymmetric cryptography 6
  authentication 6
  authorization 6
  availability 6
  brute force 6
  Cipher 6
  code injection 6
  confidentiality 6
  crack 6
  decryption 6
  Denial-of-service (DoS) 7
  dictionary attack 7
  Distributed denial-of-service (DDoS) 7

V

validation tests 14
values, method profiling tool
  exclusive time 31
  inclusive time 31
verify() method 114
ViewAsserts class
  about 98
  assertBottomAligned() method 98
  assertGroupContains() method 98
  assertGroupNotContains() method 98
  assertHasScreenCoordinates() method 98
  assertHorizontalCenterAligned()
      method 98
  assertLeftAligned() method 98
  assertOffScreenAbove() method 98
  assertOffScreenBelow() method 98
  assertOnScreen() method 98
  assertRightAligned() method 98
  assertTopAligned() method 98
  assertVerticalCenterAligned() method 98
  URL 98
VirtualBox
  URL, for downloading 125
vulnerabilities, Intents
  Intent spoofing 46
  unauthorized Intent receipt 46
vulnerabilities, smartphone 18
vulnerability
  about 8, 9
  buffer overflow 10
  cross-site scripting (XSS) 10
  improper authentication 9
  Input validation 10
  SQL injection 10

W

waitForIdleSync method 96
when() method 114
white-box tests
  about 12, 84
  basis path testing 13
  control flow testing 13
  data flow testing 13
  statement coverage 13
Wireshark
  about 123
  URL 66
  URL, for downloading 124

X

X.509 certificate
  issuer 67
  serial number 67
  signature algorithm 67
  subject 67
  subject public key 67
  validity 67
  version 67

Thank you for buying
Testing and Securing Android Studio Applications

About Packt Publishing

Packt, pronounced 'packed', published its first book "*Mastering phpMyAdmin for Effective MySQL Management*" in April 2004 and subsequently continued to specialize in publishing highly focused books on specific technologies and solutions.

Our books and publications share the experiences of your fellow IT professionals in adapting and customizing today's systems, applications, and frameworks. Our solution based books give you the knowledge and power to customize the software and technologies you're using to get the job done. Packt books are more specific and less general than the IT books you have seen in the past. Our unique business model allows us to bring you more focused information, giving you more of what you need to know, and less of what you don't.

Packt is a modern, yet unique publishing company, which focuses on producing quality, cutting-edge books for communities of developers, administrators, and newbies alike. For more information, please visit our website: www.packtpub.com.

About Packt Open Source

In 2010, Packt launched two new brands, Packt Open Source and Packt Enterprise, in order to continue its focus on specialization. This book is part of the Packt Open Source brand, home to books published on software built around Open Source licenses, and offering information to anybody from advanced developers to budding web designers. The Open Source brand also runs Packt's Open Source Royalty Scheme, by which Packt gives a royalty to each Open Source project about whose software a book is sold.

Writing for Packt

We welcome all inquiries from people who are interested in authoring. Book proposals should be sent to author@packtpub.com. If your book idea is still at an early stage and you would like to discuss it first before writing a formal book proposal, contact us; one of our commissioning editors will get in touch with you.

We're not just looking for published authors; if you have strong technical skills but no writing experience, our experienced editors can help you develop a writing career, or simply get some additional reward for your expertise.

Android Studio Application Development

ISBN: 978-1-78328-527-3   Paperback: 110 pages

Create visually appealing applications using the new IntelliJ IDE Android Studio

1. Familiarize yourself with Android Studio IDE.

2. Enhance the user interface for your app using the graphical editor feature.

3. Explore the various features involved in developing an Android app and implement them.

Android Security Cookbook

ISBN: 978-1-78216-716-7   Paperback: 350 pages

Practical recipes to delve into Android's security mechanisms by troubleshooting common vulnerabilities in applications and Android OS versions

1. Analyze the security of Android applications and devices, and exploit common vulnerabilities in applications and Android operating systems.

2. Develop custom vulnerability assessment tools using the Drozer Android Security Assessment Framework.

3. Reverse-engineer Android applications for security vulnerabilities.

Please check **www.PacktPub.com** for information on our titles

Learning Pentesting for Android Devices

ISBN: 978-1-78328-898-4   Paperback: 154 pages

A practical guide to learning penetration testing for Android devices and applications

1. Explore the security vulnerabilities in Android applications and exploit them.

2. Venture into the world of Android forensics and get control of devices using exploits.

3. Hands-on approach covers security vulnerabilities in Android using methods such as Traffic Analysis, SQLite vulnerabilities, and Content Providers Leakage.

Android Application Programming with OpenCV

ISBN: 978-1-84969-520-6   Paperback: 130 pages

Build Android apps to capture, manipulate, and track objects in 2D and 3D

1. Set up OpenCV and an Android development environment on Windows, Mac, or Linux.

2. Capture and display real-time videos and still images.

3. Manipulate image data using OpenCV and Apache Commons Math.

4. Track objects and render 2D and 3D graphics on top of them.

Please check **www.PacktPub.com** for information on our titles

www.ingramcontent.com/pod-product-compliance
Lightning Source LLC
Chambersburg PA
CBHW060143060326
40690CB00018B/3959